FOUNDATION TRUSTEESHIP
Service in the
Public Interest

by
JOHN W. NASON
for the
COUNCIL ON FOUNDATIONS

© DEMCO, INC.— Archive Safe

New York • 1989
THE FOUNDATION CENTER

The Foundation Center, established in 1956, is the only national nonprofit clearinghouse for information on foundations and foundation grants. The Center gathers and disseminates information on private giving and nonprofit activities through a wide range of reference publications and on-line database services as well as a nationwide network of library collections offering reference and educational services.

The Council on Foundations is a membership organization that serves the professional interests of over 1,100 grantmakers throughout the U.S. and overseas. Formed in 1949, today the Council's membership includes independent foundations, community foundations, corporate grantmakers (direct giving programs and foundations), public foundations, operating foundations, and foreign foundations. The Council's five goals are to: secure and maintain public policy supportive of philanthropy, promote responsible and effective philanthropy, enhance the understanding of organized philanthropy in the wider society, promote the growth of organized philanthropy, and support and enhance cooperation among grantmakers.

Library of Congress Cataloging-in-Publication Data

Nason, John W.
    Foundation Trusteeship : service in the public interest / by John
    W. Nason for the Council on Foundations.
        p.   cm.
    Bibliography: p.
    Includes index.
    ISBN 0-87954-285-3 :
    1. Endowments—United States.   2. Directors of corporations—
United States.   3. Charitable uses, trusts, and foundations—United
States.   I. Council on Foundations.   II. Title.
HV97.A3N35   1989
361.7'632'0973—dc19   88-38128

Contents

Foreword

The cover of the September 8, 1986, issue of *Business Week* was headlined "A Job Nobody Wants." The article went on to suggest that the trouble faced by members of a corporate board of directors can outweigh the honor of membership. We have not yet reached a similar state of affairs on foundation boards, but being a foundation trustee is no longer a job everybody wants. The climate for trusteeship has changed considerably in recent years. Increased dependence on the nonprofit sector has brought with it increased visibility and exposure for those who manage and distribute tax-exempt funds.

I first became a foundation trustee in 1970. It was one year after the dramatic congressional hearings on foundation performance. It was a time in which Americans were looking at both public and private organizations and asking three basic questions about them: (1) what social good do they serve, (2) to whom are they accountable, and (3) what standards are used to decide between public and private interests?

These concerns have come to focus in a very special way on foundations. Those of us who serve on foundation boards are not only stewards of foundation assets, but also custodians of a tradition and purveyors of a set of values, each of which is fundamental to a democratic society. Thus, when public judgment comes, it is only appropriate that we be expected to give an account of our stewardship in each of these areas.

Assaults on the public trust by highly placed Americans are vividly portrayed almost daily in the press. So far, the public skirmishes have not been about foundations, but we ignore allegations about uses of the charitable deductions for highly questionable purposes at our own peril. As we have learned from congressional hearings and news stories over the years, no foundation is an island. We are all affected by even the appearance of impropriety on the part of any one of the tax-exempt organizations that come close to crossing the fine line that separates legitimate and questionable practices.

Thus, this is an especially propitious moment for both foundation trustees and staff to take a hard new look at the roles and responsibilities of foundation boards. This work by John Nason started out as a revision of his earlier study, *Trustees and the Future of Foundations*, but it soon became obvious that a full reassessment was in order and that John Nason was the person to do it. His classic study of college and university trusteeship published in 1975 for the Association of Governing Boards and revised in 1982 is but one of the many examples of his skills as a dispassionate observer and insightful commentator on the performance of trustees. As Robert Goheen said in the foreword to the 1977 study, John Nason "respects facts and has no hesitation about presenting them as they are, without subterfuge or apology, as he makes his own reasoned judgement."

As a former chairman of the board of the Edward W. Hazen Foundation and a trustee for eight years of the Danforth Foundation, John Nason is soundly qualified to offer practical guidance to foundation trustees as well as carry out independent, knowledgeable inquiry. His illustrious career also includes service as chairman of the advisory committee of the Exxon Education Foundation and as president of Swarthmore and Carleton Colleges.

While this is in many ways a new report, we gratefully acknowledge the foundations that provided funding for the earlier study that served as a springboard—i.e., Carnegie Corporation of New York, Cummins Engine Foundation, Exxon Education Foundation, Maurice Falk Medical Fund, General Service Foundation, Paul and Mary Haas Foundation, Charles F. Kettering Foundation, Lilly Endowment, Inc., New York Community Trust, Rockefeller Brothers Fund, and Russell Sage Foundation.

John Nason is gracious in acknowledging the contributions of the Council staff who provided data and comments that he found helpful, but we are in his debt for the many ways in which they learned from both his patience and wise counsel. What we are most pleased about, however, is that this is John Nason's report, his conclusions and convictions, his facts and findings. More than 100,000 foundation trustees and a wide variety of other foundation stakeholders are the beneficiaries of the insights of a very wise and knowledgeable observer of the practices of foundation trustees. There is much here to help guide the way to effective foundation performance both now and in the years ahead.

James A. Joseph
President and Chief Executive Officer
Council on Foundations

Preface

Trustees and the Future of Foundations was published by the Council on Foundations in 1977. It was an attempt to examine the role and responsibilities of foundation trustees at a time when foundations were still reeling from the congressional hearings of the 1960s and the traumatic Tax Reform Act of 1969. It was based on eighteen months of field work, which involved 200 interviews with trustees and staff of every kind of foundation in every part of the country.

The present study is a major reassessment of the responsibilities of foundation trustees eleven years later. No new field work has been undertaken, but data have been brought up to date through the excellent publications of the Foundation Center and the Council on Foundations. The increasing commentary during the past decade on foundation practices and prospects has provided new insights and led me to modify some of the earlier judgments. The chapter topics in this new volume are much the same; their treatment is fresh and different.

I am indebted to Loren Renz, director of research at the Foundation Center, whose knowledge of the foundation universe saved me from many errors; to Elizabeth Boris, Alice Buhl, John Edie, and Tom Fox, vice presidents of the Council on Foundations, who made helpful suggestions chapter by chapter; to Carol Strauch, director of the Council's Information Services, whose constant and efficient assistance made the writing of this book a pleasure; and to the many wise commentators on the foundation scene, among whom Alan Pifer and Paul Ylvisaker are preeminent.

J.W.N.
Crosslands
Kennett Square, Pennsylvania
March 1988

CHAPTER 1

The Foundation Universe: Expanding or Contracting?

The Ford Foundation . . . is a large body of money completely surrounded by people who want some.

DWIGHT MACDONALD*

One clear sign of the lack of public understanding of foundations is the widespread belief that there is a monolithic sameness to them, when, in fact, few types or organizations are as varied as they are in every respect.

PETERSON COMMISSION REPORT

According to the *National Data Book* (12th edition, 1988), there are 25,639 active grantmaking foundations in the United States. These foundations hold combined assets of $103 billion, and their annual grants run just over $6 billion.[1]

A foundation, for our purposes, is a nonprofit, nongovernmental organization that makes grants in support of charitable, educational, religious, cultural, or other activities serving the public good. It has its own assets or capital fund (often supplemented by current gifts) from which grants are made. If the foundation

---

* The sources of the quotations heading this and subsequent chapters are to be found on page 151.

[1] The data used by the Foundation Center in its invaluable publications, such as *The Foundation Directory*, the *National Data Book*, *Foundations Today*, and the *Foundation Grants Index*, are based on information provided to the Internal Revenue Service by foundations. These reports range from 1984 to 1986. Since assets vary with the stock market, it is reasonable to assume that they were significantly higher at least in the first half of 1987.

is founded by a single donor or family or company, it is classified by the Internal Revenue Service (IRS) as a private foundation. If funds are provided by multiple donors, it is a public charity in IRS eyes and enjoys, as we shall see, freedom from some of the restrictions under which private foundations operate. Community foundations belong in this category.[2]

Private grantmaking foundations divide into those established by a single donor or family, often designated independent foundations, and those established by a company, usually called company-sponsored or corporate foundations. The former can be further subdivided into foundations that only make grants (the great majority) and those that primarily support and manage their own programs of research, publication, or community service— i.e., operating foundations.[3]

The following table gives a breakdown by category.

AGGREGATE FOUNDATION ASSETS AND GRANTS

Type	Number	Percent	Total Assets $(000's)	Percent	Total Grants $(000's)	Percent
Independent	24,712	96.4	91,350,303	89.5	5,484,328	91.0
Private Operating	677	2.6	6,665,405	6.5	252,746	4.2
Community	250	1.0	4,049,033	4.0	289,762	4.8
Total	25,639	100.0	102,064,741	100.0	6,026,836	100.0

Source: *National Data Book*, 12th edition, the Foundation Center, 1988. Dollar figures are expressed in thousands. The independent category includes company-sponsored foundations, of which the Foundation Center estimates there are over 1,500. No one seems to know the exact number.

---

[2] In recent years the term "foundation" has come to be used for other than grantmaking agencies. The University of Minnesota Foundation, e.g., is the channel through which alumni and friends contribute to the university. The Prince Edward School Foundation was established to provide funds for a "white only" school when the public schools in the county were desegregated. The C. Riddick McMillan Foundation International is a business enterprise. The picture is further confused by the IRS's habit of including many nongrantmaking 501(c)(3) organizations as private foundations. (See Kathleen M. Hallahan's article "The Great Numbers Debate" in *Foundation News*, July/August 1983. No wonder the general public becomes confused.)

[3] The considerable number of operating foundations that make no grants are excluded from the study.

If we look at foundations not by type, but by size of assets, we get the following table:

AGGREGATE FOUNDATION ASSETS AND GRANTS

Asset Size $	Number	Percent	Total Assets $(000's)	Percent	Total Grants $(000's)	Percent
$100 million +	148	0.6	57,784,730	56.6	2,455,839	40.7
$50 mil.–99,999,999	129	0.5	8,810,567	8.6	458,001	7.6
$10 mil.–49,999,999	846	3.3	17,394,617	17.0	1,151,249	19.1
$5 mil.–9,999,999	815	3.2	5,761,451	5.6	439,996	7.3
$1 mil.–4,999,999	3,739	14.6	8,317,352	8.1	744,424	12.4
$500,000–999,999	2,653	10.3	1,873,329	1.8	232,040	3.9
$250,000–499,999	3,065	12.0	1,095,962	1.1	166,721	2.8
$100,000–249,000	4,357	17.0	706,686	0.7	135,901	2.3
$50,000–99,999	2,733	10.6	198,096	0.2	69,144	1.1
$25,000–49,999	2,184	8.5	79,641	0.1	50,382	0.8
$10,000–24,999	1,947	7.6	32,767	—	36,726	0.6
Under $10,000	3,023	11.8	9,539	—	86,408	1.4
Total	25,639	100.0	102,064,742	99.8	6,026,836	100.0

Source: *National Data Book,* 12th edition, 1988. Dollar figures for assets and grants are expressed in thousands.

This table displays the wide range in foundation size and draws attention to the large number of quite small foundations. In a sampling of small foundations in the late 1970s, David Freeman, president of the Scherman Foundation and former president of the Council on Foundations, found "that the small foundation is, in fact, very small! In our sample the typical foundation gave away in 1977 a total of $12,000 in 12 grants, principally to educational, religious, and service organizations in its community."[4] The discrepancy between large and small foundations can be clearly seen by drawing the line, as *The Foundation Directory* does, at $1 million in assets or $100,000 or more in annual grants. By these criteria and based on estimates reported in the 11th edition of the *Directory,* 5,148 foundations, or 20 percent of the foundation world, hold 97 percent of the assets and make 92 percent of foundation grants. These are the foundations included in the *Directory.*

---

[4] "Personality Traits of Small Foundations," in *Foundation News,* September/October 1980.

Independent Foundations

Of the 25,639 active grantmaking foundations, over 90 percent are independent foundations. *The Foundation Directory*, which, as just noted, includes the top 20 percent, lists 4,100 independent foundations, with total giving (grants, scholarships, and program amounts) of $3.72 billion. These foundations, representing only 16 percent of the entire foundation universe, account for 62 percent of the $6 billion of total foundation grants. Most of the largest grantmaking foundations are independent foundations. Ten have assets in excess of $1 billion, including the Ford Foundation with assets of $4.759 billion.

Independent foundations can be divided into general purpose and special purpose foundations. The former, as the name suggests, have a broad mandate—to promote in one way or another the welfare of mankind. Most of the large foundations belong in this category. They are less likely to be family controlled and, for the most part, are managed by competent professional staff. Special purpose foundations may be either large or small. By the donor's mandate or by subsequent decision of the trustees, the foundation concentrates on limited objectives, such as cancer research, scholarship programs, or the welfare of a social group or geographical community.

Small, private nonoperating foundations are often described as family foundations, for they represent an extension of individual or family philanthropy. Grants are often made out of principal, which usually gets replenished when funds run low. Some family foundations have very distinguished records, and many of the larger foundations have grown out of small family beginnings.

Operating Foundations

Operating foundations, in contrast to independent foundations, direct most, if not all, of their income to the support of their own programs. The J. Paul Getty Trust, e.g., with assets over $3 billion, maintains seven operating programs in the visual arts and related humanities, including the renowned J. Paul Getty Museum. The Russell Sage Foundation and the Twentieth Century Fund are widely known for their research and publications in the fields of social, economic, and political policies. There are 1,818 such foundations, 1,141 of which do not make any grants and are therefore excluded from the Foundation Center's *National Data Book*. Listed by the IRS as private foundations, they also enjoy freedom from some of the restrictions imposed on private foundations in general.

Company-sponsored Foundations

Company-sponsored foundations, the number of which the Foundation Center estimates to be over 1,500, serve chiefly as conduits for corporate philanthropy. The majority receive funds from company profits in good years and distribute the money in the form of grants and financial aid. A few corporate foundations, however, have developed substantial endowments, five having assets in excess of $100 million (Alcoa, General Motors, AT&T, Ford Motor, Prudential).

Corporate giving tends to be viewed by company officers and directors as an aspect of community relations, with grants to scholarship programs for employee children and to hospitals, recreational facilities, and United Ways in communities where large numbers of employees live. Over 50 percent of corporate philanthropy is made directly by the parent company, sometimes in the form of donated services and equipment.

In general, corporate philanthropy has become more sophisticated and more significant as American business has come to recognize its share of responsibility for the public welfare. The 11th edition of *The Foundation Directory* lists 781 company-sponsored foundations, and nearly one-fourth of the 1,000 largest grantmaking foundations are company-sponsored. They have the advantage over direct corporate philanthropy of compensating for fluctuations in profits, thereby permitting a more stable and long-run program of grantmaking, and of placing a significant share of corporate philanthropy in the hands of individuals whose primary responsibility is to develop and maintain carefully thought-out patterns of giving.

Community Foundations

Community foundations are a special breed. Their assets consist of an aggregation of funds and trusts for the benefit of a specific community or region, often with donor advice or restriction as to specific purpose or beneficiary. These assets are managed either by local trust companies or by an independent board of directors, and grants are made either by the board or by a distribution committee. Often some, if not all, of the members of the board or distribution committee are appointed by local officials or agencies. Since community foundations receive their funds from multiple sources, they are considered by the IRS to be "public charities" and are not subject to many of the restrictions imposed on private foundations. *The Foundation Directory*, 11th edition, lists 160 that meet its criteria, ten of which have assets of $100 million or more. The Cleveland Foundation goes back to 1914. The New York Community Trust has assets of $527 million and makes annual grants of $42 million. Community foundations are currently the fastest growing segment of the foundation universe.

Foundation Role in Philanthropy

Foundation grants constitute a small part of American philanthropy. The estimates for 1987 are given in the following table:

1987 GIVING ESTIMATES[5]

	$	Percent
Individuals	76.82 billion	82.00
Bequests	5.98 billion	6.38
Foundations	6.38 billion	6.81
Corporations	4.50 billion	4.80
Total	93.68 billion	100.00

However small foundation giving may seem in the total philanthropic picture, grants amounting to $6 billion make a world of difference to almost every aspect of American life. In summing

---

[5] See *Giving USA*, 1988, published by the American Association of Fund-Raising Counsel's AAFRC Trust for Philanthropy. *Giving USA* includes company-sponsored foundation giving under corporations rather than under foundations.

up 30 years of experience with the Carnegie Corporation, Alan Pifer concludes

> that the funds they have available for expenditure are a particularly precious resource to the society. This is not because of their size, since the funds are quite small, but because they are constantly replenishable pools of organized and uncommitted money that can be freely, and if need be, quickly deployed to meet existing or new social needs. There are no other funds like them in the society.[6]

Pifer's statement hints at some of the reasons so many philanthropically minded people have chosen to channel their philanthropy through foundations. They want continuity and flexibility. In many instances they want continued family involvement. They recognize that foundations permit gifts that they could not as individuals take as charitable deductions—grants to students and scholars, to foreign charities, to non-501(c)(3) organizations.[7]

The many advantages of a foundation wisely managed will become evident in the following chapters. At this stage it suffices to point out that the value of foundations to the quality of American life is out of all proportion to their 6.9 percent share in American philanthropy.

Prospects for the Future

In recent years some foundation watchers have become concerned that foundations may become dwindling rather than constantly replenishable pools of philanthropy. They point to the declining birth rate of new foundations after 1969. The following table gives the figures for those foundations included in *The Foundation Directory:*

---

[6] Alan Pifer: *Speaking Out: Reflections on 30 Years of Foundation Work,* Council on Foundations, 1984, p. 7.

[7] "A private foundation is a special way to make charitable giving a creative experience; it permits the founders to establish their own agenda; it allows the flexibility to change directions to meet changing conditions; and it educates younger family members on the positive stimulation that comes with producing a better community. Finally, a foundation maintains total control of the grant-making process. . . ." David R. Frazer: "Of Lasting Duration," in *Foundation News,* January/February 1988, p. 29.

FOUNDATION FORMATION BY DECADE

Date	Number	Percent
Before 1900	42	0.8
1900–1909	20	0.4
1910–1919	73	1.4
1920–1929	156	3.0
1930–1939	190	3.7
1940–1949	708	13.8
1950–1959	1,593	30.9
1960–1969	1,156	22.4
1970–1979	627	12.2
1980–1986	446	8.7
Data not available	137	2.7
Total	5,148	100.0

The period from the end of World War II to the 1969 Tax Reform Act saw the greatest growth in the number of foundations, with the peak coming somewhere in the 1950s. These were the years of high income and estate taxes. These were also years in which foundations enjoyed relatively few governmental restrictions and were seen by donors and their lawyers not only as channels for philanthropy, but also as useful devices for maintaining control over family businesses, preserving readily accessible capital, and fulfilling other nonphilanthropic functions.

The foundation climate changed with the passage of the 1969 Tax Reform Act, which imposed a variety of restrictions and requirements on private foundations—some quite legitimate and some unnecessarily punitive. The worst features have been modified by subsequent legislation, but the accounting and reporting requirements have been a deterrent to small foundations (mostly unstaffed), and the limitation on gifts of appreciated property to private foundations has discouraged the creation of large foundations during the donor's lifetime.[8] Since 1970 approximately 10,500 foundations (nearly three-fifths in the five years following the 1969 Tax Reform Act) have terminated—a few because the donor established them for a limited number of years, some

---

[8] Since 1969 living donors could deduct only cost plus 60 percent of gain when making gifts of appreciated property to private foundations. Since 1987, the donor can deduct only cost. However, the full market value of gifts of publicly traded stock can be deducted in most cases.

through merger with other foundations (mostly with community foundations), and many because the paperwork required by the 1969 Tax Reform Act was deemed excessive.

The contributors to an important recent study, *America's Wealthy and the Future of Foundations*, view foundation prospects with some concern.[9] Teresa Odendahl and Elizabeth Boris indicate that current donors are finding alternatives to private foundations for their charitable funds, such as direct contributions to existing agencies, charitable trusts, community foundations, etc. Francie Ostrower reports that lawyers and other advisers to the wealthy have overreacted to recent tax laws and IRS regulations and tend to recommend against private foundations as instruments for philanthropy. The real problem, however, is the change in uninflated dollars of total foundation assets and the ratio of total foundation grants to the total economy. In an analysis of 937 foundations with assets of $5 million or more between the years 1962 and 1982, Gabriel Rudney found that an annual growth rate of 5.7 percent, when it was adjusted for inflation, became virtually zero. And Ralph Nelson, in a study of foundation grants in relation to gross national product for the same 20-year period, concluded that "the growth rate in real foundation grants was from one-half to two-thirds that of the general economy."[10]

A more encouraging picture is presented by Thomas R. Buckman, president of the Foundation Center, and Loren Renz, editor, in the 11th edition of *The Foundation Directory*. They point out in the introduction that the total number of grantmaking private foundations has remained relatively constant over the past decade, while the number qualifying for inclusion in the *Directory* has steadily increased. This discrepancy is attributed in part to the creation of new foundations; in part to inflation, which has effectively lowered the threshold for inclusion in the *Directory;* and in part to the stock market surge of the 1980s, which has enhanced the dollar value of foundation assets. One positive trend

---

[9] Edited by Teresa Odendahl, sponsored by the Council on Foundations and the Yale University Program on Non-Profit Organizations, published by The Foundation Center, 1987.

[10] *America's Wealthy*, p. 131.

identified in the *Directory* is a resurgence in the rate of foundation formation—74.3 per year in the 1980s compared with 62.7 per year in the 1970s.

Buckman and Renz further point out that while *Directory* foundation assets grew from $24 billion in 1969 to $89.9 billion in 1985 in current dollars, they grew from $24 billion to $27.9 billion in constant dollars, a growth of 16.2 percent. Although assets declined in constant dollars between 1972 and 1981, they made a substantial recovery from 1981 to 1985. During the period 1972–1985, foundation giving in constant dollars increased 32 percent, much of it occurring in the years 1981–1985.

The most recent data are encouraging. The Council on Foundations has mounted an aggressive campaign to publicize the advantages of foundations. Large foundations have recently been created, such as the John D. and Catherine T. MacArthur Foundation, the AT&T Foundation, and the Fred Meyer Charitable Trust; and existing foundations have had substantial increases to their assets—e.g., the J. Paul Getty Trust and the Horace W. Goldsmith Foundation. On the other hand, some provisions of the Tax Reform Act of 1986 have potentially damaging consequences for philanthropy in general and for the creation of new foundations.

Charitable trusts have existed in this and other countries for several centuries. Charity in the form of grantmaking foundations, however, is largely an American phenomenon of the twentieth century, which is now spreading to many other countries. In spite of its many critics, it has been an extraordinary success. Foundations will presumably grow and flourish if they continue to serve the public welfare well. In the United States that decision will depend on the collective action of 150,000 individual foundation trustees.

CHAPTER 2

Trustees:
Private Almoners or
Public Servants?

This is my money and it's nobody's business how I give it.

ANONYMOUS TRUSTEE

But philanthropy is far more than grantmaking; it is a constitutional statement by society that there should be a private counterpart to the legislative process, a freestanding alternative that allows for independent considerations of the public interest and private allocations of resources for public needs.

PAUL YLVISAKER

Central to any understanding of the role of foundation trustees is the issue of whether they are spending or giving away strictly private money or money in which in some sense the public has an interest or claim. Are foundations merely a systematic way of carrying on the personal charitable interests of the donor or donors? Or does the public, whose welfare is presumably being served by foundation grants, have some sort of vested interest in how the money is spent? How do trustees balance their responsibility to honor the donor's intent and their responsibility to safeguard the best interests of the beneficiaries?

Foundations as Personal Charity

It is easy to follow the reasoning of those who insist that foundation grants are a form of personal giving. People of wealth, having made or inherited their money, are free to spend it as they

11

wish, subject to payment of taxes and avoidance of illegal activities. Theirs is the choice to devote it to houses and horses, to the support of relatives and friends, to making more money, to homes for stray animals, or for the glory of God. Most people do not question their right to give to college A rather than to university B, to religion rather than to art museums, or to organizations bolstering the status quo rather than to agencies seeking to change our society. On what grounds, then, should anyone seek to limit the exercise of their private preference if and when they elect to systematize their philanthropy through the establishment of foundations? Have not they and their trustee successors the same unfettered right to direct foundation expenditures to whatever institutions and causes they personally prefer?

The persuasiveness of this position is strengthened when we consider the preponderance of small family foundations in the foundation universe. Twenty thousand foundations, or 81 percent of the total have less than $1 million in assets, while 10,458, or 42 percent have less than $100,000. Even though many receive annual gifts, which are then passed along in the form of grants, the number and size of the grants are small and reflect very clearly the preferences of the donors.

Public Character of Foundations

At the other extreme are those who claim that foundation funds are public money, meaning that they are virtually the same as government money. Much of the money used to establish or enlarge foundations, the amount depending on the tax code at the time, would have ended up in government coffers if it had not been diverted for foundation purposes. By legislative fiat, it is left under private rather than government control.

Attacks on foundations from the far left have often stemmed from this allegedly anomalous situation. The more extreme attacks hold that all tax exemption for charitable contributions is wrong, as was occasionally voiced in the 1986 tax reform hearings. The public welfare is the responsibility of the Congress, which is composed of representatives elected by the people; it is not the privilege of a self-perpetuating group of wealthy individuals. A more moderate view is held by those who recognize the value of private foundations but argue that the public aspect of their funds justifies much greater public control over their operations and particularly over their boards of trustees.[1]

The Modern Foundation's Dual Character

There are at least two reasons why the view that foundation assets are government money is mistaken.

(1) If tax exemption is merely a way of distributing responsibility for spending government money, the argument applies to all nonprofit organizations and not just to foundations. It transmutes all private college and university endowments, all private hospitals and museums, the entire rich plethora of nonprofit agencies into government funds and operations. They may be left undisturbed in private hands for much of the time, but when questions arise, the government would have every right to intervene. The truth is that foundation funds are not public funds or government money in the sense that the appropriations to Health and Human Services out of tax revenues are held and allocated by civil service staff employed by the government. They are as private as the endowments of Stanford University, the Menninger Clinic, and the Metropolitan Museum of Art. Just as the trustees of those institutions have the responsibility of managing the funds in conformity with their respective charters, so do the trustees of charitable trusts, which include foundations, have the clear obligation of carrying out the terms set forth in the founding instruments.

(2) The argument puts the cart before the horse. Foundations are not government money thinly disguised because their assets were tax deductible and their income (largely) tax exempt. They are given these tax privileges because they are dedicated to serving the public good. While tax deductions have undoubtedly stimulated the establishment of many large foundations, it is worth

---

[1] A thoughtful elaboration of this general philosophy is to be found in the position of the National Committee for Responsive Philanthropy. See, e.g., the testimony of its executive director, Robert O. Bothwell, before the House Subcommittee on Taxation and Debt Management, February 24, 1984.

remembering that 146 foundations, including Carnegie and Russell Sage, were created before there was any income tax. Milton Katz has stated the foundation's dual nature well: "The foundation is public because it devotes all its resources exclusively to educational, scientific, religious, charitable, or other public purposes and applies none of its resources to the pecuniary advantage of any person (other than regular compensation for services rendered). It is private in the sense that it is non-governmental and derives its resources from gifts by private donors (or income from the investment of such gifts). *It is a privately organized public institution.*"[2]

The Constitution of the United States, now 200 years old, requires the government to promote the general welfare of the people. From the beginning, however, Americans have supplemented governmental action with generous private philanthropy. Foundations are an important part of that effort, not because they are so large, for we have seen that they constitute a small fraction of American philanthropy, but because of their multiplicity, their freedom from the constraints of government and of the market place, and their commitment to the public welfare, however that may be individually conceived. If we genuinely believe in the plurality of the public and the private sectors, we must defend foundations against the encroachment of government. And, paradoxically, that defense involves the recognition that, since foundation activities are intended to enhance the public good, the public has a legitimate concern in how foundations operate, particularly in how they determine what is the public good.

For family foundations with limited funds, this presents no great problem. Neither foundation donor nor foundation beneficiary sees a significant difference between a check from the donor's private account and a check from his or her foundation. But for the middle-sized and large-sized foundations, the issue is central. "What is at stake here," writes David Truman, trustee of the Twentieth Century Fund, "is not fiduciary obligation in the usual

---

[2] *The Modern Foundation; Its Dual Character, Public and Private,* The Foundation Center, 1968. Italics added.

sense of respect for the testamentary wishes of the donor, but rather the very possibility of the disposition of resources through autonomous bodies such as foundation boards. Unless the latter fully accept, and are seen to accept, the 'public servant' concept, they will be destroyed or taken over by the government."[3]

---

[3] Private letter to the author.

CHAPTER 3

Programs by Default or by Design

Wealth is nothing new in the history of the world. Nor is charity. But the idea of using private wealth imaginatively, constructively, and systematically to attack the fundamental problems of mankind is new.

JOHN W. GARDNER

Foundations change, like it or not. The fundamental issue is whether they will change by chance or for significant reasons. The latter comes about only through conscious effort.

FREDERICK deW. BOLMAN

It is easy to give money away; it is hard to give it intelligently. In spite of his gifts of libraries across the country and other benefactions, Andrew Carnegie found that he was making money faster than he could spend it and so established the Carnegie Corporation, thereby setting an example for American philanthropy throughout the current century. Another businessman, the founder of the Charles A. Dana Foundation, put it this way: "There is no question in my mind that it is easier to earn money and amass a considerable fortune than it is to make charitable investments [i.e., grants] that are always intelligent."[1]

Throughout mankind's history, the act of charity has been an emotional response to a need or demand that touches our hearts. The term *philanthropy*, however, suggests a more thoughtful ap-

---

[1] *Thirty Years 1950–1980 & Annual Report 1980*, the Charles A. Dana Foundation.

proach. James A. Joseph, president of the Council on Foundations, found this to be true in his study of the origins of the
generous impulse. "For many of the people I have studied," he
wrote, "there was a basic difference between philanthropy and
charity. Philanthropy for them was more cognitive; it involved
thought before action. Charity, on the other hand, was more
affective; it grew out of an emotional feeling that led to a more
spontaneous response."[2]

In his usual perceptive manner, John Gardner points to the
unique opportunities that foundations provide. They can set up
systematic and coherent programs. They can make long-term
commitments to remedying problems that will not respond to
short-term efforts. They are flexible in meeting new demands and
new needs. They can afford to take risks that public agencies
would find too controversial. They can, and do, provide relief for
suffering; but they can also study and attack the root causes of
the ills of our society.

However, not all of them do so. An intelligent and coherent
program of giving is the result of careful planning. Donor or
trustees must determine goals or purposes.[3]

For small family foundations, which constitute, as we have
seen, the bulk of the foundation world, planning is a minimal
exercise. For the most part their guidelines are set by the donor's
educational, religious, cultural, medical, and community concerns. Even in these foundations, however, one of the incen-
tives—probably the major one—is to avoid the pressure to make
hasty decisions at year end. The result is more thoughtful giving.

---

[2] *Foundation News,* September/October 1986, p. 45.

[3] Note the resolution adopted in 1971 by the board of the Carnegie Corporation:
"A primary responsibility of the board of trustees of Carnegie Corporation of
New York is to focus its attention on the effectiveness of the Corporation's
program as a whole, from a policy standpoint. While retaining final grantmaking
authority, the board should play a greater role in setting, reviewing, and revising
the broad objectives of the Corporation than in scrutinizing individual proposals
for grants. It should be concerned with the distribution of the Corporation's
resources among the general areas of philanthropy chosen by the Corporation
at any time, and with the questions of whether those areas are of critical and
continuing importance in the society." Quoted by Caryl P. Haskins in his article
"A Foundation Board Looks at Itself" in *Foundation News,* March/April 1972,
p. 14.

Special Purpose Foundations

It is a different story when we move up the scale to the middle- and large-sized foundations, those, e.g., that qualify for inclusion in *The Foundation Directory*. Many of these, including some of the largest, are restricted to a specific purpose or field by the donor or by the board of trustees. Consider the following examples.

The Robert A. Welch Foundation of Houston, Texas, is now one of the 50 largest foundations with assets around $240 million. It was established by bequest in 1954. In his will Mr. Welch wrote:

> I have been spared to live beyond the alloted span of three score years and ten, and, in that lifetime, by hard work and sacrifice, assisted to some extent by good fortune, have accumulated property of substantial value. My desire, now, is to make that disposition of it by will which will result in its being used in the way most beneficial to Mankind. I have long been impressed with the great possibilities of the betterment of Mankind that lay in the field of research in the domain of Chemistry. This is a feeling that I think is widely held by others. It is a popular expression to say that we are living in a "Chemical World." Day by day we see marvels wrought in that field.

As a result, "the general policy of the Foundation is to support long-range fundamental research in the broad domain of chemistry within the State of Texas only."[4]

The Spencer Foundation, established in 1962 in Chicago, Illinois, has current assets around $200 million. In a memorandum written shortly before his death, the donor said:

> All the Spencer dough was earned, improbably, from education. It makes sense, therefore, that much of this money should be returned eventually to investigating ways in which education can be improved, around the world. Broadly conceived, wherever learning occurs.[5]

The Elsa U. Pardee Foundation, incorporated in 1944 in Midland, Michigan, which has current assets around $25 million,

---

[4] *Annual Report*, 1974–1975, Robert A. Welch Foundation, p. 9.

[5] *1986 Annual Report*, The Spencer Foundation, p. 3.

restricts its giving to the cure and control of cancer. Grants are limited to hospitals, universities, and institutes for cancer research and control.

In some cases the trustees, rather than the donor, have designated the specific purposes to which grants will be restricted. Neither John nor George Hartford, who left their large holdings in the Great Atlantic and Pacific Tea Company to the Hartford Foundation, laid down any requirements as to program. The trustees were responsible for limiting the program to medical research. The Independence Foundation in Philadelphia, a splitoff from the old Donner Foundation, concentrates on the support of private secondary education as the result of deliberate trustee decision.

The role of the trustee is somewhat less demanding in special purpose than in general purpose foundations. But it is not easy to spend wisely $10 million per year in the field of chemistry, especially when spending is limited to Texas scientists and institutions. The improvement of education around the world is a tall order. Even in the cure and control of cancer, tough decisions must be made regarding which researchers, which institutions, and which lines of investigation to support. It is not often that a donor will be as specific as James Buchanan Duke. The trust instrument (1924) of the Duke Endowment gives as its purpose: "To make provision in some measure for the needs of mankind along physical, mental, and spiritual lines"; but, in fact, Mr. Duke restricted the program to North and South Carolina and specified the minimum percentage of income to be given to Duke University, Furman University, Johnson C. Smith University, Davidson College, private hospitals, orphanages, rural Methodist churches, and ministerial pensions. Even so, with annual grants of $40 million, the trustees of the Duke Endowment still have difficult and far-reaching decisions.

General Purpose Foundations

The charters of most foundations are written in broad terms in order not to limit the purposes that trustees may want to pursue someday. The Rockefeller Foundation was created in 1913 to further "the well-being of mankind throughout the world." The senior Mr. Rockefeller, however, was convinced that health was the key to well-being, with the result that the foundation concentrated in its early years on programs of science and medicine. The improvement of medical education throughout the world and the demonstration of the value of public health programs are monuments to a brilliant program of well-organized and consistently sustained philanthropy.

The trustees of the Ford Foundation, when they finally geared up for action in 1950, adopted the report of the Gaither Committee, which based its recommendations on the premise:

> In the Committee's opinion the evidence points to the fact that today's most critical problems are those which are social rather than physical in character—those which arise in man's relation to man rather than in his relation to nature. Here, it was concluded, is the realm where the greatest problems exist, where the least progress is being made, and where the gravest threat to democracy and human welfare lies.[6]

As a result, the trustees focused for some years on the problems of democracy, world peace, the economy, education, and the scientific study of man. In subsequent years the program was revised as new presidents took over the leadership of the foundation.

The trustees of the Fred Meyer Charitable Trust in Oregon have chosen to divide the income from their $250 million in assets between "general purpose grantmaking, believing that such a flexible and varied approach is beneficial in an area with relatively few foundations" and concentration on one or more specific fields where "thoughtful, sustained attention to a specified set of problems can have significant long-range results."[7] Currently the Trust emphasizes two such programs: "Preserving the Future: Support for Children at Risk" and "Aging and Independence."

---

[6] *Report of the Study for The Ford Foundation on Policy and Program,* The Ford Foundation, 1949, p. 14.

[7] See Charles S. Rooks, executive director: "Developing a Grantmaking Program" in *Foundation News,* November/December 1987, pp. 60–63.

These are but three examples of the kind of thoughtful planning required by large general purpose foundations. It should be obvious that the larger the foundation, the more important planning becomes. A $5-million grant program will usually have a far more significant impact than one of $5,000. And the more general the mandate of the foundation, the more imperative it is for trustees to select those areas of activity in which foundation support will concentrate. Not even the largest foundation can respond adequately to all requests, however worthy and legitimate they may be; and the broader support is spread, the greater the danger of "scatteration," that ever-threatening blight to sensible philanthropy. Broad general purposes are by no means the monopoly of the larger foundations, however. The fact that one's funds are modest is all the more reason for deciding how to make them more effective.

Continuity versus Change

There is no point to fashioning a program unless one is prepared to stay with it long enough to see results. The early Rockefeller Foundation program in medicine and public health, already referred to, is a good example. The magnificent study of higher education in the United States, the most comprehensive ever made, by the Carnegie Commission on Higher Education (1967–1973) and by the Carnegie Council on Policy Studies in Higher Education (1973–1979), is another. The long-term goal of the Robert Wood Johnson Foundation is improved health and health care for all Americans. After 15 years of emphasis on access to primary medical care for the general population, the foundation now proposes to focus on assistance to groups most vulnerable to illness, on disease of regional or national concern, and on broad issues such as the quality and equity of health care.[8]

The world, however, does not stand still. The fundamental problems of mankind may remain the same, but the social, eco-

---

[8] See "On Building a Foundation," by David E. Rogers, M.D., president of the Robert Wood Johnson Foundation during the period, in *Foundation News*, July/August 1987; and the Robert Wood Johnson Foundation's 1987 annual report.

nomic, and political contexts in which they manifest themselves do not. One of the great dangers of any institution is rigidity. It is easier to stay in the same rut than to carve out a new path. The wise trustee knows that boards and institutions grow stodgy and complacent and that a periodic renewal of vision and purpose is essential to foundation health.[9]

How and when should this review be made? Often the appointment of a new CEO provides the occasion for a reassessment of old programs and a fresh consideration of new ideas. Two considerations led the Bush Foundation to review its program in 1982: first, the need to reconfirm or redesign several programs, the funding of which was scheduled to end in the 1980s; second, the realization that a majority of the trustees had not been on the board when the programs were initiated in the early 1970s. The Geraldine R. Dodge Foundation decided to emphasize a major program of support for the study of Chinese as a result of a review in 1982 of their 50 most successful grants "with an eye toward selecting a fresh, major initiative of national interest." Incidentally, in view of the fact that half the world will be speaking Chinese by the year 2000, this may prove to be one of the more dramatic and constructive contributions to the future of the United States.[10]

Some foundation boards make it a practice to set aside one meeting a year to discuss ends and means in place of the usual foundation business. Or special meetings can be scheduled every three or five or ten years. The review can be done internally at minimum cost in dollars and considerable cost in staff and trustee time. An outside consultant can be brought in, as suggested by the Council on Foundation's Self Study Program. A committee of interested and knowledgeable experts is a more expensive but often highly productive way of getting new perspectives.

---

[9] See John Gardner: *Self-Renewal*, Harper and Row, 1963, for an excellent treatment of the tension between continuity and change in institutions.

[10] See Humphrey Doermann: "Long-Range Planning: Facing Reality," in *Foundation News*, May/June 1986, for the Bush Foundation story; and Rose L. Hayden: "Helping Teach the Unteachable," in *Foundation News*, November/December 1987, for more details about the Dodge Foundation.

Foundations do change. Thomas Parrish gives an amusing illustration in his essay, "The Foundations: 'A Special American Institution'":

> According to some authorities, the first United States foundation was the Magdalen Society of Philadelphia, a perpetual trust which exists today as the White–Williams Foundation. Its aims have been somewhat modified from those it was given in 1800, which were "to ameliorate the distressed condition of those unhappy females who have been seduced from the paths of virtue and are desirous of returning to a life of rectitude." After more than a century of patient attempts to keep going in the face of the chronic insufficiency of unhappy females desirous of rectitude and of the frequent intractability of those who did present themselves, the trustees voted in 1918 to broaden the work of the foundation.[11]

One need only look at the Rockefeller, Ford, Northwest Area, Wieboldt, Mary Reynolds Babcock, Charles F. Kettering, and many other foundations—large, middling, and small—to find excellent examples of honest review and intelligent renewal.

There remain, however, too many foundation boards that ignore the need for periodic reassessment of goals, too many trustees who seem to think that they are reviewing the foundation's program every time they make a grant, too many whose concept of their role as trustees is reflected in the comment of the man who said, "I like being a foundation trustee. It gives me an opportunity to make all my friends happy."

It would certainly do no harm, and it could do a lot of good, if every foundation trustee were to articulate briefly and clearly what he or she conceives to be the purpose and the strategy of the foundation. A comparison of such statements by trustees on the same board might produce a vigorous and salutary discussion. Good foundation practice requires in its own self-interest something more in the way of review than mere lip service. Effective management requires more. The shifting forces affecting public welfare require more. Trustees would do well to listen to the wise

---

[11] Fritz Heimann (ed.): *The Future of Foundations*, p. 13.

valedictory comment of John D. Rockefeller III upon his retirement from the board of The Rockefeller Foundation:

> I cannot emphasize too strongly the need for constant critical review of programs and a continuing willingness to re-examine established assumptions. In my opinion, terminating programs that have, so to speak, completed their mission, is often as difficult— and necessary—as the wise selection of new programs. In both cases, flexibility as to change is the basic requirement.[12]

Company-sponsored Foundations

American corporations gave $4.5 billion in 1987 to a variety of charitable causes, and just under $1 billion of this amount was channeled through the 1,500 or so company-sponsored foundations. Why do so many corporations continue to use their foundations for charitable giving, since the current excise tax on foundation income and other complications favor direct giving? For those with substantial endowments, the answer is clear, but there are only 88 foundations with assets of $10 million or more. There are a number of reasons. Foundations stabilize company giving by evening out the fluctuations in annual earnings. They provide better management by putting responsibility for corporate giving on the shoulders of designated staff and directors. They permit better program development by providing scope for long-range plans.

The best of the company-sponsored foundations are managed in a thoughtful, sensitive, and responsible manner, with much care given to a carefully thought out and articulated program. The Exxon Education Foundation is widely admired for its support of education. For 42 years the Dayton Hudson Corporation has given directly and through the Dayton Hudson Foundation 5 percent of pretax income to arts and social action programs. Most company-sponsored foundations focus on the problems and needs of the communities where they do business; others are reaching out to embrace national and even international concerns. Self-interest plays a natural part in corporate philanthropy.

---

[12] Quoted in *Foundation News*, November/December 1971, p. 237.

Texaco's underwriting of the Metropolitan Opera's Saturday after-noon broadcasts is good public relations as well as a fine public service. B. Dalton Bookstores' support of literacy programs a few years back was a significant contribution to a society with the highest level of functional illiteracy in its history; it was also a natural for a bookseller.

Studies by the Conference Board and others have not given the general run of company-sponsored foundations high marks for their giving programs. Narrowly viewed as a form of advertising or public relations, often treated as a necessary but inconvenient accessory, they were—and some still are—inadequately managed. That situation has been changing, with a new climate of concern for public and social issues and a new sense of responsibility for careful planning.[13]

Community Foundations

The problem of establishing a rational program is both simpler and more acute for the boards of directors or the distribution committees of community foundations. Many of the individual funds or trusts that constitute the assets of community foundations have designated purposes and beneficiaries; with occasional ex-ceptions, all the resources are intended to serve a given com-munity, county, or state. This seems much simpler than the promotion of the welfare of mankind. Needs, however, always outrun resources. Decisions have to be made—on a haphazard system or on the basis of a well thought out plan.

The older and larger community foundations are well managed, and some of the newer ones exhibit considerable imagination and vitality. Many, however, are struggling to achieve a program, badgered on the one side by a constant stream of heart-rending requests for help and handicapped on the other by boards not able or not willing to make the kind of decisions out of which a responsible program is created.

---

[13] See the excellent articles by Peter Hutchinson, chairman of the Dayton Hudson Foundation in *Foundation News*, January/February and September/October 1987; and the Council on Foundation's Occasional Paper No. 3, *Community Change/Corporate Responses*, January 1987.

CHAPTER 4

The Hard Choice Among Competing Needs

Any individual can waste his substance in riotous living if he so desires . . . But if a foundation is to be true to the only proposition that can serve as a sound rationale for its existence, it simply does not have the liberty to waste its resources. No matter that foundations do not always live up to what they should stand for, the philosophy that undergirds them must maintain that they exist, along with government, to tackle and try to solve the major problems of the society.

MERRIMON CUNINGGIM

Our principal and overriding priority as trustees of grantmaking and grant-receiving organizations will be to participate aggressively in the process that will determine what this society will be like in the 1990s. To discharge that obligation, we will have to operate constantly as risk takers—as movers and shakers if you will—a characteristic for which we have not been particularly noted in the past.

JOHN H. FILER

The raison d'etre of foundations is to serve the general welfare by making grants for charitable, educational, religious, scientific, cultural, and other purposes. Since needs always exceed resources, tough decisions must be made among valid, and often moving, appeals for foundation help.

How will trustees make those tough decisions? What criteria will they use? Which purposes will they elect to support: relief

27

of suffering or study of the causes of social problems; well-established institutions (colleges, universities, hospitals, museums) or newly fledged social-action agencies; or preservation of the existing order or social change?[1]

The tumultuous changes of the last half century and the troubled condition of the times make the choices both more difficult and more important.

Degrees of Difficulty

The trustees of small family foundations may feel that they do not face such a wide range of decisions—partly because the funds at their disposal are limited and partly because the foundations were created to carry on preexisting family philanthropies. Nevertheless, some serious thought is in order. New conditions create new pressures and new needs. "The range of opportunities open to even the smallest foundation," writes David F. Freeman in his highly useful *Handbook on Private Foundations,* "is so great that the process of solution among worthwhile undertakings can become an exciting challenge."

Trustee decisions are also limited in those foundations that have been committed to special purposes. If that commitment was made by the trustees, it can, of course, be changed; a responsible board of trustees will periodically review its past decisions. If the commitment was made by the donor in the foundation's charter, the trustees have no choice. But, in both cases, trustees will have to decide which agencies and which programs within the given purpose will best fulfill that purpose, and these may well change from time to time. Consider the examples cited in chapter 3: the trustees of the Robert A. Welch Foundation must make annual

---

[1] Consider Alan Pifer's comment: "There is, in truth, little agreement on the social purposes foundations should serve. Some would say that the test of good performance in foundation grantmaking is its impact on 'social change,' others whether its funds offer 'empowerment' to powerless groups in the society, others the level of support it gives to critically important institutions and organizations, others whether it serves as a fountainhead of new ideas or new solutions to old problems, others whether it has the capacity to exert leverage of substantial sums of public money, others whether it carries out whatever mission its trustees have agreed upon—be it restoring Civil War monuments or promoting excellence in violin playing." *Speaking Out: Reflections on 30 Years of Foundation Work,* 1984, Council on Foundations, p. 10.

grants of $10 million within the state of Texas for research in chemistry. The trustees of the Spencer Foundation must spend $5 million annually for the investigation of learning and the improvement of education throughout the world. The expenditure process is no easy matter.

In theory, the trustees of company-sponsored foundations have wide latitude in the choice of ends. In practice, however, as noted earlier, they tend to be guided by what will be good for the company. Even within this philosophy their decisions are not easy, as the problems of the communities they serve or in which their employees live are changing and complex.

It was suggested in the previous chapter that community foundations face an easier problem than other types of foundations because they consist for the most part of a congeries of earmarked funds. While all funds are earmarked for a given community or region, not all are limited to specific beneficiaries. The closeness of the community foundation to the multifaceted problems of the community presents difficult and often agonizing decisions to the trustees or the members of the distribution committee. The best of the community foundations will have a comprehensive understanding of the needs—and of the politics—of the community. As such, they can serve both as a resource to other foundations with less expertise and as a rallying point for a joint research approach to a given problem.

Patterns of Foundation Philanthropy

The introduction to *The Foundation Directory* contains a section on trends in foundation giving that deserves thoughtful examination by all foundation trustees. The following table, taken from the 11th edition of the *Directory*, gives a summary picture:

FOUNDATION GIVING TRENDS*

Category	Percent						
	1980	1981	1982	1983	1984	1985	1986
Cultural activities	13.5	15.3	14.0	15.4	14.0	14.6	14.7

* These percentages are based on the grant records of 459 foundations sampled. Although they represent only 1.8 percent of the foundations and 44 percent of foundation grants, they probably reflect reasonably accurately the distribution of foundation grants in general.

Category	Percent						
	1980	1981	1982	1983	1984	1985	1986
Education	22.4	21.3	23.9	16.0	17.4	16.8	21.9
Health	25.1	22.5	20.9	21.7	23.7	23.5	20.5
Religion	2.4	2.0	1.9	2.1	2.3	1.9	1.3
Science	6.4	6.9	6.5	9.0	7.5	8.9	6.4
Social science	5.7	6.0	6.9	7.4	7.6	8.3	8.8
Welfare	24.5	26.2	25.9	28.4	27.5	27.2	26.4

Paul Ylvisaker presents a more detailed analysis over a longer time span in chapter 20 in *The Nonprofit Sector: A Research Handbook,* already referred to, and he draws a number of interesting conclusions. Among them is the following:

> Admittedly, there are disparities between potential and performance. *In the aggregate,* foundation giving has favored the *more established* agencies, *conventional* fields of interest and modes of operation, and *more advantaged* constituencies. . . . Foundations collectively have not responded with great agility or countervailing force to shifting public needs and patterns of financial support. Nor has the *net* activities of foundations over time served significantly to reduce disparities between rich and poor, majorities and minorities—as one might expect of philanthropy, given its original conception. But given also the massiveness of modern society and the resistant forces at work, all that may be too much to expect of foundations whose resources are so comparatively tiny.[2]

It is of some interest to compare these figures with the distribution of total U.S. philanthropy as summarized in the latest edition of *Giving USA* (1987). Exact comparison is difficult, as the *Directory,* Ylvisaker, and *Giving USA* use different systems of classification.

TOTAL U.S. GIVING BY RECIPIENT CATEGORY

Category	$ Amount (in billions)	Percent
Religion	$43.61	46.55
Health	13.65	14.57
Education	10.84	11.57
Human services	9.84	10.50
Arts, culture and humanities	6.41	6.84
Public/society benefit	2.44	2.60
Other	6.89	7.35
Total	$93.68	100.00

[2] Yale University Press, 1987, p. 374.

Since there is never enough money to satisfy all requests, trustees must be selective in making grants. Inevitably there will be criticism of the way grants are distributed. Many criticisms will be reactions to disappointment, but others will reflect divergent social and political philosophies inherent in a democratic society. These need careful attention.

Are Foundations Too Liberal?

From time to time, critics of foundations allege that foundation money is being used to support subversive agencies or programs, partisan political activities, or programs undermining capitalism and the American system of free enterprise. In 1952, the Cox Committee held congressional hearings on such charges. It found so few examples of what it considered improper activities that it concluded with an endorsement of the role of foundations. Not content with this assessment, Representative Reece of Tennessee in 1954 charged on the floor of the House, "Some of these institutions support efforts to overthrow our government and to undermine our American way of life." His committee hearings were a one-sided farce. The committee brought in a divided report, which the minority attacked as an "unseemly effort to reach a predetermined conclusion."[3]

To some extent, the extensive hearings conducted by Representative Wright Patman in the 1960s reflected the same ultra-conservative concerns, mixed incongruously with Patman's own belief that foundations represented powerful and dangerous tools of the economic elite.

Many foundations have made grants for liberal causes, the Ford Foundation being an outstanding example among the big foundations. The standard justification for foundations, repeated almost ad nauseam, is their freedom to explore and to experiment, to try out new ideas, to point the way to a better society. If support for social change and social justice undermines the American way

---

[3] These events are described in the Report of the Commission on Foundations and Private Philanthropy (the Peterson Commission) entitled *Foundations, Private Giving, and Public Policy,* chapter 7.

of life, then foundations can be subversive. Indeed, since the early 1970s there has appeared a number of "alternative" foundations—Vanguard, Haymarket, Bread and Roses, Liberty Hill, Crossroads Fund, and others—committed to social justice and the redistribution of economic power. Partly because of their influence, there has developed a National Network of Grantmakers consisting of 300 or so foundation executives of "mainline" foundations, who share some, although not all, of the alternatives' concerns.

Therefore, it is not surprising that the 1980s have seen a resurgence of conservative concern in some foundation quarters. In addition to the inevitable conservative dislike of what is seen as the liberal trend of foundations, some foundations have become distinctly vocal in support of capitalism and their interpretation of American democracy. In this group are to be found the John M. Olin, Smith Richardson, Sarah Scaife, and the newer Bradley Foundation. Although fewer in number than the alternative foundations, they hold and dispense vastly more money. They join forces in the Institute for Educational Affairs, described by its president, Leslie Lenkowsky, as "the conservative interest group in the philanthropic world."

Foundations exist because the structure and principles of American society have enabled donors to accumulate excess capital. It is natural for donors and the trustees who represent them to view with suspicion and alarm actions that seem to threaten the system by which they flourished. Human nature being what it is, the conservatives' criticism of the main body of foundation giving is likely to continue.

Are Foundations Too Conventional?

Concerned over the criticisms of foundation practice that surfaced during the Patman hearings, the Peterson Commission made a study of the giving record for the years 1966–1968 of a cross section of American foundations. Finding only 0.1 percent of the grants to be "controversial" and 3 percent to be "innovative," the Commission concluded, "A majority of foundations spend most of their funds on conventional projects and in conventional ways that are similar to the traditional patterns of individual giving."[4]

This charge has been repeated again and again in the publications of the National Committee for Responsive Philanthropy, a Washington-based group advocating more philanthropic and foundation attention to newly formed, usually powerless, and unconventional segments of society. A study of Oregon foundations in 1981 revealed that over 50 percent of their grants went to just 30 institutions (including eleven colleges and universities, three hospitals, three art institutions, and one museum), whereas barely 1 percent of foundation dollars supported programs run by or for racial minorities. In San Diego, a similar study found that 2.1 percent of grants went to ethnic and racial minority organizations, although minorities comprised 21.4 percent of the county's population. In Minnesota, the Philanthropy Project, a Twin Cities research and advocacy group, reported in 1987 that "Minnesota's largest foundations bolstered funding for the disadvantaged from 28 percent in 1982 to 30 percent in 1984 and to a healthier 38 percent in 1985."[5]

Conventional philanthropy is important. Colleges and universities, art museums, symphony orchestras, and a wide panoply of service agencies could not exist without it. The criticism is not that foundations support conventional institutions and causes, but that they support them to the exclusion of new and unconventional agencies.[6]

---

[4] Page 86.

[5] See *Oregon Foundations: Private Sector Responses to Public Needs; Report on San Diego Foundations; Responsive Philanthropy,* Summer 1987. Much the same picture is presented in other NCRP studies, such as *What Kinds of Groups Receive Colorado's Foundation Grants?;* the Bay Area Committee for Responsive Philanthropy, *Small Change from Big Bucks;* the D.C. Community Support Fund, Inc., *Where Did All the Money Go?, An Inside Look at Foundations and United Ways.*

[6] "Nevertheless, with all the money you invest in DNA research, Stanford Business School, and chamber groups that play Scarlatti," writes Charles Merrill, "give some thought to the needs of black women prisoners at the absolute bottom of society who grope for something better out of life for themselves and their children." *The Checkbook,* Oelgeschlager, Gunn & Hain, 1986, p. 260. Subtitled *The Politics and Ethics of Foundation Philanthropy,* this book tells the story of the Charles E. Merrill Trust. The section on pages 18–27 and the final chapter, "How It Adds Up," are an entertaining and at times frightening account of the way the trustees decided on grants.

Are Foundations Too Conservative?

This is the real thrust of the National Committee for Responsive Philanthropy and its local committees. Restriction to conventional funding identifies foundations as defenders of the status quo. What about their opportunity to improve social justice? What of their unique capacity to support new ideas, new experiments, new solutions? "For an institution that presumes to be society's conscience, gadfly, critic, and innovator," write Paul Ylvisaker and Jane Mavity, "private philanthropy's performance (even friends and practitioners will admit) has generally been less than bold."[7] A few foundations have taken the lead in exploring the possibilities of social change.

The Ford Foundation has already been mentioned. The New World Foundation, as well as the new alternative foundations, belong here. In 1986 the Public Media Center in San Francisco published an *Index of Progressive Funders* listing 130 foundations and other philanthropic agencies representing over $100 million in grants to advocacy and social change institutions.

Foundations have been faulted for their disregard not only of the inarticulate and helpless members of society, but also of the major problems that threaten the survival of society. In his most recent book, *The Golden Donors,* a study of the performance of the 36 foundations with assets of $250 million or more, Waldemar Nielsen concludes, "With the exception of a splendid minority, our largest foundations are not even attempting to grapple with the major and most threatening problems confronting the nation and the world at the present time."[8] He lists "three glaring examples"—the areas of war, peace, and national security; the degeneration of the productivity and competitiveness of the American economy; and the emerging crisis of the overburdened and underperforming American welfare state.

Nielsen ends on a note of subdued optimism. He believes that government regulations have done about all they can. Reform

---

[7] "Private Philanthropy and Public Affairs," in *Research Papers,* sponsored by The Commission on Private Philanthropy and Public Needs, 1977, vol. II, p. 821.

[8] Page 425.

must come from within, encouraged by challenging appraisals from thoughtful critics. He writes:

> As this process proceeds, ignorant, amateurish, and petty philanthropy, which still characterizes a good part of the activity of even the very large foundations, should become an early casualty. Random small institutional support grants, passivity in grantmaking, and confinement of the work of a large foundation to purely local matters will more and more clearly be seen as lost opportunities, as a failure of awareness and vision. The surest antidotes to inconsequential grantmaking are better information and open debate. The influence of such exposure may work somewhat slowly and unevenly, but it is already beginning to be felt.[9]

Foundation Role in Public Policy

Foundation support for the study of any one of Nielsen's three overarching problems would precipitate the involved foundations into public policy debates. Recommendations to heighten national security, to improve the American economy, or to revise health care would immediately engender fierce discussion, and they would quite properly be the subject of controversy. In general, foundations can seek to relieve suffering, support research (including education and the arts), and examine the structure and operation of society—political, economic, and social—in the hope of finding better policies for serving the public good and enhancing the welfare of mankind. In the long run, the most important of these is the study of public policies.

Some foundation trustees prefer to avoid public policy issues, partly because they think they may be subjecting themselves to penalties under current tax laws. They point to the recurrent charges in congressional investigations that foundations have had a subversive influence or have sought to influence legislation.

The 1969 Tax Reform Act specifically approved foundation involvement in nonpartisan public policy issues, but equally clearly ruled out foundation participation in political campaigns and in any lobbying expenditures and a clearer distinction between permissible and impermissible lobbying. Lobbying in self-defense was

---

[9] Page 431.

reaffirmed. Technical advice to a governmental body upon request was permissible. Nonpartisan analysis, study, or research was allowed.

There the matter stood until 1987, when the IRS finally announced a series of proposed regulations redefining lobbying so as to include the use of foundation-sponsored research by a third party for lobbying purposes to hold the original foundation responsible, and to make penalties retroactive to 1976. The Council on Foundations, the Independent Sector, and other nonprofit organizations staged so vigorous a protest that the IRS agreed to reconsider the proposed regulations. While the final outcome has not yet been determined, the ability of private foundations to fund public policy activities will survive.[10]

"Among the most difficult and important issues facing foundations," writes Alan Pifer, "is the question of the legitimacy and feasibility of their participation in public policy formation. In this function is to be found what is very possibly the most substantial opportunity foundations have today for service to the nation but also, perhaps, their greatest vulnerability." After examining the policy of caution, he goes on to say:

> An alternative and more persuasive view, which some foundation trustees and administrators hold just as strongly as the apostles of low-profile cautiousness hold theirs, is that the only ultimate protection for foundations is to remain relevant, necessary institutions—whatever the risks entailed. The best way for foundations to do this is to be constantly sensitive to public policy issues in the fields in which they operate and not be afraid to initiate or support activities that relate to these issues. Indeed, the greatest justification for foundations continuing to enjoy tax-exempt status lies in their making the maximum contribution they can, within their spheres of influence and competence and within the limits of the law, to the development of enlightened public policy for the nation.[11]

---

[10] See *Foundation News,* March/April 1985 for two interesting articles—"Foundations and Public Policy: Coming of Age in the 1980s," by Frank Karel, and "Influencing Public Policy: The Legal Limits," by John Edie. These plus other useful information are to be found in the Council's Resources for Grantmakers Series' "Foundations and Public Policy." The issue is discussed further in chapter 12.

[11] "Foundations and Public Policy Formation," in *Philanthropy In An Age of Transition,* 1984, pp. 105, 107–8.

Concluding Thoughts

The choice among competing needs in American society, let alone throughout the world, is legion. They range from local self-help organizations to global disarmament. In addressing such a wide array, foundations have two major advantages: their number and variety, and their freedom as private sources of support for public purposes. Within the terms of their charters and the tax laws, foundation trustees may use their own best judgment, and the survivability of foundations in the long run will depend on how good that judgment is.

For many, perhaps most, trustees the choice of ends is limited, as we have seen, by donor priorities and by limited funds. For the rest, however, and they control most of the foundation money, the choice is wide open. Boards of trustees have been largely composed of people of wealth and their close associates. Their framework of values is largely set by their position in society. The ultimate question is whether enough of them can rise enough of the time above that framework and their own vested interest in maintaining the status quo to recognize the forces changing our social institutions and structure. Will enough of them recognize the claims of a changing set of public needs and be prepared to use some of the resources at their disposal to help a different world take shape or to insure that some world survives? In highest terms, this is the challenge of statesmanship—of the capacity to see beyond self to the good of all society.

In reflecting on the role of foundations at the end of 40 years of service on the Rockefeller Foundation board, John D. Rockefeller III commented:

> The uncertainties and urgencies of our time make it essential for every institution concerned with public service to re-examine its approach. Foundations particularly must constantly strive to attain their full potential in helping to deal with the critical problems and issues that confront us . . . *I think that most foundations are too cautious in their approach—too prone to concentrate their efforts in areas of the tried and proven.* There has never been a time in our history when we were confronted with problems of the complexity and magnitude that we are today. If these problems are to be resolved, I believe that every element in our society must do its part. To mea-

sure up to this challenge we in the foundation field must be willing
to innovate, to take risks, to make mistakes.[12]

It will also be a matter of prudence, for if too many people feel
left out of the system, sooner or later they will seek to change
the system. This is the stuff that revolutions are made of.[13]

---

[12] *Foundation News*, November/December 1971, p. 237.

[13] See Thomas R. Asher: "Public Needs, Public Policy, and Philanthropy," a
critique of the Filer Commission report, especially the conclusion, published by
the Department of the Treasury, 1977, *Research Papers*, vol. II, part II, pp. 1069–
1092. Or listen to the rhetoric of Vernon Jordan in an address to the Foundation
Luncheon Group in New York in June, 1972: "It is obvious that the searing,
urgent issues currently tearing at the fabric of our society, require for their
resolution institutional changes that will enlarge the opportunities and the role
of the neglected minority segments of our nation. These questions constitute a
challenge of the first magnitude to the foundation community, a challenge that
calls its very being into question. For if foundations refuse, either through fear
or through misunderstanding, to try to resolve these burning issues, then they
are truly a redundant and expensive luxury in our society." Searing, urgent
issues continue to plague our society, and it is encouraging to note that Vernon
Jordan, by subsequently serving on the Rockefeller Foundation board, and more
recently on the boards of the Taconic and Ford Foundations, apparently believes
foundations can do something about them.

CHAPTER 5

Board Composition

The trustees . . . have the ultimate decision-making powers over what grants are to be made or withheld. Their general orientations are thus the major determinants of the foundation's policies and its impact on the cultural scene. That is, they are important gate-keepers of ideas.

LEWIS A. COSER

Beyond these practical approaches to the problem of partisan bias in grantmaking, probably the only protection available to a foundation lies in having a diversified board of trustees and staff in which a reasonably wide variety of experience in the nation's life is represented. If there is too much homogeneity in a foundation's management—homogeneity of occupational or professional background, economic status or interest, social perspective, or political persuasion—there is likely to be no one involved at the critical moment of decision to challenge the assumptions underlying a proposed course of action.

ALAN PIFER

No one knows how many foundation trustees there are; estimates range from 100,000 to 230,000.[1] The correct figure is probably

[1] In her chapter in *America's Wealthy*, already cited, Elizabeth Boris concludes that the average foundation has four trustees, which gives a total of 102,556 trustees for 25,639 foundations. The Council on Foundations found an average number of eight in its most recent (1988) management survey. That would yield 205,112 trustees, but its sample is based on a limited number of relatively large foundations, most of which are staffed. The foundations listed in the eleventh edition of *The Foundation Directory* average six trustees for each of the 5,148 foundations included in the book. This makes for a total of 153,834 trustees, which is a figure that is probably closer to the fact than either extreme mentioned earlier in this note.

in the neighborhood of 150,000. This group of individuals controls the disposition of $6 billion—a modest part of total American philanthropy, as we saw in chapter 1, but nevertheless a substantial sum, which is crucial to the health and survival of the myriad nonprofit agencies and organizations that shape our society. Collectively, the members of this group give the foundation world its character and carry the responsibility for its performance. Foundations will be judged by the decisions trustees make.

Profile of Foundation Trustees

Who are these 150,000 individuals whose decisions carry such weight? What kind of people are they? How do they view their world? Recent surveys by the Council on Foundations of its members and the members of various regional associations of grantmakers give the following figures:

FOUNDATION BOARD DEMOGRAPHICS*

	Percent		
	Private	Community	All
Male	71	71	71
Female	29	29	29
White	95	92	94
Black	3	6	4
Other	2	2	2
Under 40	11	9	10.1
41–50	19	23	19.8
51–60	31	36	32.3
61–70	25	26	25.5
Over 70	14	6	12.2

More women serve on the boards of small private foundations (under $10 million) than on the boards of foundations of $100 million and over, 33 percent for the smaller, 17.7 percent for the larger. There is no significant variation on the boards of community foundations. With respect to minority trustees, the largest foundations, both private and community ($100 million and

---

* Gender and race figures are to be found in the Council's *1988 Foundation Management Report.* Data on age of trustees are taken from the Council's *1980 Trustee Report.*

over), have a higher percentage (8.8 percent) than the smallest foundations (4.4 percent).

The most recent information on the occupations of foundation trustees is to be found in the Council's *1980 Trustee Report.*

OCCUPATIONS OF FOUNDATION TRUSTEES

	Percent		
	Private	Community	All
Law	15	18	15.9
Banking	11	13	11.5
Business	39	43	40.6
Education	13	5	10.6
Medicine	4	4	3.9
Foundation	2	1	1.6
Volunteer, housewife, community service	7	10	7.4
Religion	9	6	8.5

Sporadic studies of foundation trustees over the past fifty years show only slight changes in the composition of foundation boards.[2] The most striking instance is in the number of women on boards. Coffman reported 2.5 percent in 1930, Andrews 7 percent in 1952. Steady pressure in recent years has brought the figure to 29 percent. In spite of growing concern for the role of minorities in our society, there has been little improvement in the number of blacks, Hispanics, and Asians on foundation boards.

In 1930 Lindeman described the typical foundation trustee as

> . . . a man well past middle age; he is more often than not a man of considerable affluence, or one whose economic security ranks high; his social position in the community is that of a person who belongs to the highest income-receiving class of the population; he is, presumably, "respectable" and "conventional" and belongs to the "best" clubs and churches, and he associates with men of prestige, power, and affluence.

---

[2] See Eduard C. Lindeman: *Wealth and Culture,* Harcourt, Brace & Co., 1936, pp. 44–46; Harold C. Coffman: *American Foundations: A Study of Their Role in the Child Welfare Movement,* YMCA New York, 1936; and F. Emerson Andrews: *Philanthropic Foundations,* Russell Sage Foundation, 1956, chapter 3. The findings of all these surveys may be distorted both by the limited base and by heavy concentration on the larger foundations.

The typical trustee today is not much different. Seventy-five percent of trustees are male, 95 percent white, 70 percent age 51 or over, 67 percent from law, banking or business, and the great majority Protestant. In an egalitarian age, where there has been erosion of the traditional patterns of authority, it is small wonder that the composition of foundation boards is a focus of attack. The criticisms take two forms—lack of healthy diversity and, second, family domination.

The Case for Diversification

Three lines of argument point up the desirability of greater diversity on foundation boards. First, too great homogeneity, as Pifer suggests in the quotation at the beginning of this chapter, tends to limit the range of viewpoints. Diverse backgrounds provide a wider range of judgment. Robert Bothwell and Timothy Saasta of the National Committee for Responsive Philanthropy argue the case in vigorous terms:

> And this insulation [from the world of grantseekers] constitutes the central paradox of foundations: that their greatest strength—their independence—is also their greatest potential weakness. This is because the frequent companion of independence is isolation. . . . First, foundation officials must be willing to enter the worlds of those whom they are trying to help. And second, they must be willing to examine the assumptions that they take with them and respect the assumptions of others within those worlds.[3]

It is not just the advocates of the underdog, however, who are concerned over the narrowness of viewpoint of the majority of foundation boards. The Report of the Peterson Commission recommended added diversity and concluded with the trenchant comment: "There is an obvious contradiction in claiming to represent the interests of pluralism in our society and yet practicing monism in the selection of trustees." And one of the recommendations of the Filer Commission runs as follows: "That tax-exempt

---

[3] "Learning to Listen," in *The Grantsmanship Center News*, January/February 1983.

organizations, particularly funding organizations, recognize an obligation to be responsive to changing viewpoints and emerging needs and that they take steps such as broadening their boards and staffs to insure that they are responsive."[4]

Greater diversity on boards does not, and should not, entail the concept of representation. Advocates of change in foundation structure sometimes talk as if foundation boards should be composed of representatives of women, minority groups, ethnic groups, the poor, the powerless, the beneficiaries—indeed, almost any distinguishable segment of society. Apart from the sheer impossibility of including representatives from all groups, the result would be boards of unwieldy size, of strongly conflicting interests, of political maneuvering, of confrontation, and finally of resolution by compromise. However inevitable or appropriate these characteristics may be to the political scene, their opposite is desirable for private boards. Apart from the donor's intent, a trustee does not "represent" anyone. He or she has responsibilities, as we have seen, both to remain true to the terms of the trust, so far as circumstances will permit, and to safeguard the best interests of the beneficiaries of the trust. Integrity and impartiality, intelligence and commitment—these are the hallmarks of the good trustee.

Is it not a contradiction in terms, it will be asked, to propose board members from diverse groups in society and to deny that they should represent the interests of those groups? The answer involves a subtle but important distinction. Experience, sensitivity, and perspective are not the same as advocacy and special pleading. We know that to be true in our own lives, and since we cannot experience all things, we need to supplement our limitations with the experience of others. Eugene C. Struckhoff, executive director of the Community Foundation of the Greater Baltimore Area, describes the distinction beautifully in his standard work on community foundations:

---

[4] *Foundations, Private Giving, and Public Policy,* University of Chicago Press, 1970, p. 138; *Giving in America,* 1975, p. 170. Consider also Ylvisaker's trenchant observation: "We are probably the most unrepresentative of American institutions"; *Foundation News,* May/June 1984, p. 44.

Every member of a board has a duty to speak to overall public interest and not for a single interest. In reality, however, each member brings to the board perceptions of priority and morality grounded in her or his life experience and condition. Boards composed only of white Anglo-Saxon Protestant males with backgrounds in business affairs and drawn from more affluent socioeconomic groups do not mean to speak only or substantially for WASPS. They may intend the public welfare; but they are handicapped in achieving it in not being exposed to the aspirations and perceptions of the many constituencies they should serve. The member of a racial minority or other group will labor under a like disability in achieving the theoretical ideal of representing only the overall public interest. The rationale for a board drawn from diverse elements is grounded in the irrefutable fact that no one can get out of his skin. Theory and reality are not at war in this instance. It is, indeed, bad policy for a board member to regard himself as speaking *for* a constituency; but it is both inevitable and right for her or him to speak *as* a member of a group.[5]

A second reason for greater board diversity is visibility and accessibility. The most monolithically structured foundation can be readily accessible to all and sundry if it so decides. But the social and economic status of the majority of trustees naturally focuses their attention on the issues and institutions with which they are familiar and conceals their availability from nontraditional and nonconventional grantseekers. This is the burden of the criticism both of the Filer Commission and of the National Committee for Responsive Philanthropy, leading to their recommendations, one as a voluntary action and the other mandatory, that foundations seek more diversified boards.

And finally, there is the political or pragmatic argument. The modern temper is suspicious of elite organizations and of what appears to be undemocratic power. It is skeptical of traditional patterns of authority and insists on greater participation in decision making by those affected by the decisions. Foundations are under attack on all these counts. The composition of their boards and their long record of privacy, now at last being modified but

---

[5] *The Handbook for Community Foundations,* Council on Foundations 1977, chapter VII, section 1.11(3).

still characteristic of the majority of foundations, lay them open to criticism. Greater board diversity would do much to improve their public image.

The Issue of Family Control

Private foundations (except company-sponsored ones) are created by individuals out of their own resources to perpetuate or expand their personal philanthropy. Except for foundations established by bequest, the donor serves on the board of trustees and normally has the dominant voice. The original board usually consists of family members and close business or professional associates who can be expected to share the donor's interests and values and to carry them on after the donor's death. Even when it is established by bequest, a foundation's original board will be determined by the donor.

Donor and/or family control have been the target of recurring criticism since the establishment of the Rockefeller Foundation in 1913. Populists have been hostile, as we have noted, to what they considered the dynastic control of great wealth. Patman uncovered enough instances of the use of foundations to perpetuate control of family businesses to justify the restrictions of the 1969 Tax Reform Act. Even trustees such as Carl A. Gerstacker, trustee of the Rollin M. Gerstacker and Elsa U. Pardee Foundations and former chairman of the board of Dow Chemical, think that family control is undesirable. In a speech to the Council of Michigan Foundations in 1975, Gerstacker said:

> First, we need to adjust our thinking to the fact that foundations are now clothed with the public interest. . . . Second, it follows, I believe, that if we are public institutions (or "quasi-public"), we should not remain strictly family boards of trustees. We need to reconstitute our boards of trustees so that a majority of the trustees come from outside the family. For many of us this may be an upsetting and controversial thought, but I am convinced that it should have the highest priority on our foundation's agenda.

For community foundations, the issue is minimal. Members of distribution committees or governing boards are often appointed by outside agencies, institutions, public officials, or trustee banks.

It is worth noting, however, that they are less broadly representative of the community than it is often assumed. According to the table on page 41, 74 percent are lawyers, bankers, or businessmen, as contrasted with 65 percent for private foundations. Community foundations do permit donor advisory funds (and some actively solicit them), in which the donor and/or individuals appointed by the donor may make nonbinding recommendations for the fund's expenditures; but this kind of "family" control terminates either with the death of the donor or with the death or resignation of those named by the donor. In all cases, however, the distribution committee has the final decision and can deviate from the donor's preference if it is considered unsuitable.

Family control is not an issue for company-sponsored foundations. Company control, however, is a natural and universal aspect of such foundations. This is not likely to change. As the social concerns of corporate officials grow, however, corporations are finding it advantageous to enrich and broaden their foundation boards by the addition of outside trustees.

Nor is the concern about donor and family control really relevant to the huge population of small family foundations. As was noted in chapter 1, *The Foundation Directory,* 11th edition, lists 5,148 foundations with assets of $1 million or more or grant programs of $100,000 and up. These represent 20 percent of the foundation universe, possess 97 percent of total foundation assets, and make up 92 percent of foundation grants. Eighty percent of the foundation pyramid consists of small, primarily family-controlled foundations making annual grants of less than $100,000. With a few exceptions, these are, in a quite literal sense, the extension of individual giving. Family decisions might be enlarged and improved by nonfamily advice, but it would be contradictory and counterproductive to eliminate family control.

The Case Against Family Control

The issue of donor and continued family control over the charitable use of foundation money focuses on the middle- and large-sized foundations. At this time there are no family members left on the boards of the Ford, Rockefeller, and Kellogg Foundations, e.g., and only one out of nineteen on the board of the Carnegie Corporation. Why is there such concern about family control in the large number of substantial foundations dominated by family board members?

The first argument is based on the advantages of diversity of viewpoints in grantmaking. There is a lot to be said for this argument, as we have seen. It has been stated in many forms, perhaps never more succinctly than in the 1965 Treasury Department Report on Private Foundations:

> Under present law it is possible for an individual to establish a private foundation, dominate its affairs throughout his life, and pass its management to members of his family upon his death. In such a system supervision of the activities of a foundation may remain within the power of a very limited and homogeneous group for an indefinite period of time; there is, indeed, no assurance that persons more broadly representative of the public will ever be introduced into the organization's governing body.
>
> The disadvantages of the system are apparent. All of the dangers of narrowness of view and parochialism can persist in perpetuity. A foundation's motive force can, over time, become dissipated; and it is not guaranteed a source of replenishment. Attitudes may harden into prejudices; approaches may solidify; the responsiveness which this branch of philanthropy should have to the changing needs of our society may suffer. Projects which were useful and desirable when they were undertaken may be continued long after they have become outmoded.

A second argument is the one already so well expressed by Carl Gerstacker in the quotation cited earlier in this chapter. Other things being equal, an institution invested with the public interest should have some public input in its management.

Those who are convinced by this line of argument have proposed various remedies. The authors of the 1965 Treasury Report would limit family and donor related trustees to 25 percent of the board after 25 years of foundation activities. The Donee Group recommended to the Filer Commission that all foundation boards be required to have one-third public members at once and two-thirds after five years. Some years back, Alan Pifer, then president of the Carnegie Corporation of New York, suggested a division between private family charities and independent foundations. The former would enjoy relatively few restrictions respecting investments, family control, and confidentiality, but their assets would be disposed of and the "charity" dissolved within ten years of the donor's death. Independent foundations would be subject to various restrictions regarding investments, to full accountability, and to the requirement that a majority of the trustees not be related to the family. Arnold Zurcher, former executive director of the Alfred P. Sloan Foundation, has advocated a distinction by size, using $2 million in assets as the dividing line between the small family foundations and "institutionally autonomous, privately governed funds for the public good." And the Filer Commission, taking a moderate middle course, recommended the following:

> That a new category of "independent" foundation be established by law. Such organizations would enjoy the tax benefits of public charities in return for diminished influence on the foundation's board by the foundation's benefactor or by his or her family or business associates.[6]

The Case for Continued Family Control

Defenders of foundations as now structured begin with the flat assertion that there is no empirical evidence proving that independently managed foundations are better run than donor-controlled foundations. No study along these lines has as yet been undertaken. In view of the subjective character of such an analysis, a persuasive study is highly unlikely. Students of foundation performance can cite shining examples and horror stories on both sides of the issue, and conclusions will differ according to the weight one puts on various examples. Under the circumstances, the burden of proof would seem to rest on the critics.

---

[6] *Treasury Department Report on Private Foundations,* 1965, p. 56; Donee Group: *Private Philanthropy: Vital and Innovative? or Passive and Irrelevant?,* pp. 17–18; Alan Pifer: *The Foundation in the Year 2000,* Foundation Library Center, 1968, pp. 9–11; Arnold J. Zurcher: "Family Foundation 'Conglomerates'—What Should We Do About Them?" in *Nonprofit Report,* April 1974, p. 13; Filer Commission: *Giving in America, 1975,* p. 172.

Second, it is maintained that the involvement of the donor and his or her family is an asset that should not be discarded. The donor brings drive and energy, as well as imagination and creativity, to the foundation he or she creates. The children and grandchildren inherit a sense of family responsibility, and as different generations join the board, differences of outlook and interest begin to appear. Some family-controlled foundations have been quite venturesome. Furthermore, the proper handling of wealth does not always come easily. It needs to be learned, and what better way to accomplish this than by serving as a trustee of one's family foundation?

But the strongest argument in favor of continued family control is based on incentive. If potential donors are denied a determining voice in the disposition of their bounty, they are unlikely to put their money into a foundation. This is simply the way human nature works. Since it is their money, it would be unreasonable to exclude them from its management. The same argument does not apply, at least with the same cogency, to the involvement of their children and grandchildren. Here again, however, motivation is an important factor. It is natural for donors to want their families to carry on their interests, and family involvement has not infrequently led to further family gifts.

Desirability of Public Members

In the preceding discussion of board diversity and of family control, reference has frequently been made to *public members,* and it is important to understand what is meant by this term. The extreme position is taken by those who insist that since foundations have been granted special benefits because they serve the public good, the public should have some voice in how the beneficiaries are selected. Thus, the National Committee for Responsive Philanthropy (successors, as previously noted, to the Donee Group) favors representatives of the public on all foundation boards; the alternative foundations (Vanguard, Bread and Roses, Haymarket, Liberty Hill, et al.) go so far as to invite distribution committee members from groups of beneficiaries.

The position taken here is that public members are individuals independent of family and immediate business associates—individuals who can and, if necessary, will challenge family assumptions, who will broaden the intellectual and cultural horizons of the board, and who will serve both as a conscience to the board and as a symbol to the public that they have a friend at court. The method of appointment to many community foundation boards is designed to achieve these goals. Such a method would be quite impractical for private foundations, the boards of which are self-perpetuating. There is, however, no reason under the self-perpetuating system not to reach out beyond family members for additional breadth of experience and wisdom, consistent with loyalty to the donor's intent.

There are other ways in which small family foundations can safeguard themselves from intellectual and cultural inbreeding. One of the simplest is through the use of outside advisers, consultants, or advisory committees. Another way is to join in a network of local or similar foundations where the viewpoints and experiences of several foundations are shared. Such associations, which can be quite informal, sometimes result in a division of responsibilities for addressing local problems.

In the last analysis, foundations should be judged on the good they do rather than on the structure or methods by which they achieve their results. After nearly 100 years of foundation experience, however, it is now becoming clear that some methods produce better results than others. And even if this were not true, it is becoming clear that the picture foundations present affects the public's and the lawmakers' judgment of their value. From time to time, proposals have been put forward that family members be mandated off foundation boards or that public members be mandated on. It would be wise to recognize the public's stake in foundation philanthropy and voluntarily take appropriate steps before being forced to do so.

CHAPTER 6

Selection, Education, and Renewal

It is increasingly clear that the effective functioning of a foundation is conditioned by the proper blending of personal qualifications and fundamental viewpoints in the team of laymen who compose the board of control.

ERNEST V. HOLLIS

A self-perpetuating board may well achieve a kind of self-satisfied insularity that almost defies attention to fundamental change in the conditions appropriate for sensible policy.

WILBERT E. MOORE

Who decides, and by what process, who shall be foundation trustees? There are three routes to board membership: designation by the donor, appointment by an outside agency, and selection by other board members.

Designation by Donor

With the exception of community foundations, the initial board is usually selected by the donor and, while he or she is alive and active, the donor's voice is likely to be decisive in the selection of successor trustees. Indeed, by restrictions in the charter, the donor can control the choice of future trustees, as in the case of the Marion I. and Henry J. Knott Foundation of Baltimore, where the articles of incorporation and bylaws limit membership to the two donors, their twelve children, and spouses and descendants of the charter members. Where the donor sets up his or her foundation as a charitable trust, the trustees are likely to be officers of the bank or trust company managing the corpus, or individuals appointed by the institutional trustee. In other cases where a highly trusted lawyer has been named by the donor to the original board, practice if not prescription has sometimes led to selection of younger partners of the law firm to succeed their seniors. A variation of this "hereditary" practice occurs when, by specific provision or by practice, a son or daughter of a trustee is nominated to succeed the parent.

The donor's desire to have descendants serve on the foundation board is readily understandable. But descendants do not always share the donor's interests and concerns. Too circumscribed a selection process can be an invitation to future problems.[1] On the other hand, too little provision for continuity of board membership can result in even greater problems. Small family foundation boards often fail to make plans in advance for their own perpetuation.

In company-sponsored foundations the donor company determines who shall recommend grants for approval. This may be the CEO, the manager of public relations, the managers of local operations, a specially chosen professional, or a committee involving one or more of the above, and sometimes others. Trustees or directors of corporate foundations may serve for fixed terms or at the pleasure of the CEO or the corporate board of directors. They are appointed by those who control the source of the funds.

---

[1] In his will establishing the Dorothy Rider Pool Health Care Trust, Mr. Pool stipulated that there should be one corporate and four individual trustees. "I direct that, at all times one of the Individual Trustees shall be a medical doctor, one shall be a business person, and one shall be an attorney at law." So far this has worked well, but it is conceivable that the time may come when the improvement of the health care of the citizens of the Lehigh Valley might be better guided by a different combination of talents. Through the trust indenture establishing the Duke Endowment, James Duke specified that the self-perpetuating board of fifteen should always contain a majority of natives or residents of North Carolina and South Carolina. By selecting as the first board a group of individuals chiefly associated with the Duke Power interests and by requiring that the assets of the foundation be invested in the Southern Power System securities, he made certain that the board would initially be dominated by individuals representing his business interests.

External Appointments

Community foundations are required by law to have "a representative governing body." Depending on how they are established, community foundations may select their own board members. For many community foundations, however, some members of their boards may be designated by the trustee banks, by outside public officials (such as the mayor or a local judge), by citizens prominent in the community (e.g., a local university president), or by agencies representing important professional, civic, or social service activities. In some instances, boards so composed have authority to co-opt other members. Appointments are normally for specific terms, i.e., five or seven years, and not infrequently a member may not serve for more than one or two successive terms.

In spite of these arrangements, or perhaps because of them, there is room for improvement in the makeup of community foundation boards or distribution committees. Outside officials often do not understand what is needed. They are often too busy to give the selection their serious attention. In time they become lax. The practice of suggesting "good" appointments to them may have the practical effect of making distribution committees self-perpetuating. Eugene Struckhoff in the *Handbook* cited previously suggests that community foundation boards should prepare careful analyses of their membership, strengths and weaknesses, duties required, and bylaws and other relevant regulations as a background for decisions by outside authorities. "The most appropriate conduct by a board seems to be to inform an appointing authority as fully as possible so that he can exercise his function intelligently . . . and, if asked, to suggest several individuals the existing board believes possess those qualities."[2]

External appointment is rare among boards of independent foundations, but it does occur. The five-member board of the Trexler Trust of Allentown, Pennsylvania, is appointed in theory by the seven judges of the Court of Common Pleas of Lehigh

---

[2] *The Handbook for Community Foundations: Their Formation, Development, and Operation,* Council on Foundations, Inc., 1977, p. VII-17.

County and in practice by the President Judge. According to the trust's secretary and chief operating officer, this system has produced a better balanced board than would self-perpetuation.

The Northwest Area Foundation, located in St. Paul, Minnesota, has a two-tier system of governance—a governing board of directors, the eleven members of which are appointed by a five-member board of trustees. The trustees are appointed for three-year staggered terms by the Ramsay County District Court. The system is cumbersome, but has so far worked well. It is potentially dangerous in that political considerations could influence the appointment of directors and thereby change the character of the foundation.

Self-perpetuation

In the great majority of independent foundations, boards of trustees are self-perpetuating, but this practice has been subject to criticism in certain quarters. To some it represents the perpetuation of power without proper public accountability. To others it is the main cause of "cronyism" and the lack of adequate diversity on foundation boards. Yet it has several practical advantages. It is an uncomplicated procedure. It allows the people who should know best what the board needs for effective functioning to make the choices. It avoids the often abrasive political debate characteristic of public bodies. It emphasizes the responsibility of trustees to the terms of the trust. Alternatives are complex and, as we have seen, not always satisfactory.

Planned Selection—Central to Success

The formal machinery for selecting trustees is one thing; the actual selection practice of many boards is quite another. While the donor is still alive, he or she may make quite arbitrary choices. In foundations with a strong family influence, new trustees, whether they are younger members of the family or outsiders, are frequently decided upon in informal family conferences. Sometimes the chairperson or a very influential trustee will assume responsibility for recommending additional members, looking upon the selection as virtually his or her prerogative. In other instances the chairperson will informally ask trustees for the names of suitable candidates, often at the last minute, and individuals so proposed are then elected without further investigation. In all these cases the formality of a board vote is honored, but the choice has been made elsewhere—sometimes with exemplary consideration of what the foundation needs, but all too often in a haphazard fashion, which gives some justification to the charge of cronyism.

The selection or appointment of board members can occur in hit-or-miss fashion or by careful planning. And since the board plays so central a role in the foundation's performance, the choice of its members is of crucial importance. The key is careful, intelligent planning. This means a nominating committee (by whatever name it may be called) whose responsibility it will be to analyze board membership in terms of skills, background, age, gender, race, and any other relevant considerations; to plan for future developments; and to generate a panel of suitable candidates. This assignment is sometimes assumed by the executive committee, but in general it is better done by a committee with a single responsibility. Arthur Frantzreb of the consulting firm of Frantzreb and Pray Associates is emphatic on the subject:

> The Committee on Trustees should rank second in importance only to the executive committee. It should define the trustee role and function, prepare and update a trustee profile, maintain lists of and research on trustee candidates (even those who may be elected), continually analyze present strengths of members, design the matching of tasks to people, design procedures for trustee enlistment and programs for trustee education.[3]

However it is done, a carefully thought-out design for the selection of new trustees is important for all foundations. It has special importance for large foundations with their wide-ranging interests. It is essential to community foundations. It has been an important factor in the success of the major company-sponsored foundations. And the smaller family-oriented foundations will profit from more thought about the composition of their governing boards.

---

[3] "Your Trustee Chairmanship: Its Position and Function," in *Fund Raising Management*, May/June 1975, p. 31.

Qualities of the Good Trustee

What qualities should a nominating committee look for? What makes a good trustee? There is no single set of answers. A family foundation needs interested family members. A community foundation needs people who know and care about the community. Special purpose foundations will seek people with competence in the area of activity. General purpose foundations will depend on breadth of view. But there are certain basic qualifications that apply to almost all trustees.

1. Interest in and concern for the foundation and its field or fields of operation. The job is too demanding for anyone who lacks a fair degree of enthusiasm for the task.
2. Some understanding of the area of the special purpose foundation and some broad perspective on the problems of society for the general purpose foundation. Eleanor Elliott of the Foundation for Child Development suggests that every trustee should be able to answer the question: "Namely: in 50 words or less, what is this place all about?"[4]
3. Objectivity and impartiality are a *sine qua non*. The board table is no place for special pleading, for temperamental bias, for personal whim. The trustee is judge, not advocate, save with respect to the donor's priorities.
4. Special skills. The board will need certain special forms of competence among its members—management, investment experience, familiarity with budgets, knowledge of the law. Not all trustees need possess all these attributes. The value of planning and of Frantzreb's analysis of current membership lies in making certain that some trustees will possess some of these special kinds of expertise.
5. A capacity for teamwork, for arriving at and accepting group decisions. Irresolvable differences, the tactics of confrontation, *ad hominem* arguments, and lack of respect for one's fellow trustees are destructive of intelligent group decisions. These qualities demonstrate the danger of diversity carried to an extreme. Collegiality in the form of uniform outlook is stultifying; collegiality as a way of disagreeing, yet working harmoniously together is essential.

---

[4] "On Being a Trustee," in *Foundation News*, May/June 1984, p. 38. An excellent article, well worth reading by every trustee.

6. Willingness to work. This means a willingness to give time and thought to the affairs of the foundation, to arrange one's personal schedule so as to be available to attend meetings, to serve on committees, to undertake special assignments, and to wrestle with the problems of the foundation.
7. Practical wisdom. This is more easily recognized than described. It involves the capacity to see the whole picture, to recognize the validity of opposing arguments, to distinguish principle from expediency, and to temper the ideal with what is realistically possible.
8. Commitment to the foundation as a whole and not to special interests or constituencies. The trustee's responsibility is to the foundation.
9. Commitment to the idea of philanthropic foundations. No foundation is an island unto itself. Every trustee, even in small family foundations, has a responsibility to act in such a way that the foundation world is strengthened and not weakened.
10. Moral sensitivity to the act of giving and to the need for giving. Paul Ylvisaker calls the latter a "sense of outrage"—outrage over people dying of cancer or of AIDS, over children born to poverty and deprivation, over the destruction of the environment, over the threat of nuclear annihilation. Merrimon Cuninggim describes the former as "the potential immorality of giving," the ego satisfaction of the giver, the corrupting influence of the sense of power.[5]

The question is sometimes raised whether foundation trustees should be specialists or generalists. In general purpose foundations either staff or consultants or advisory committees should be relied on for professional or technical knowledge. In special purpose foundations it is probably desirable to have some trustees with special competence in the foundation's restricted field. By and large, however, foundations will be better served by men and women of vision and imagination, people who can bring dispassionate, objective, and broadly based judgments to bear on foundation policies and issues. One argument for "men of affairs" (of either sex) on foundation boards is their breadth of view and

---

[5] Paul N. Ylvisaker: "Is Philanthropy Losing Its Soul?" in *Foundation News,* May/June 1987; Merrimon Cuninggim: *Letters to a Foundation Trustee,* Center for Effective Philanthropy, 1986, p. 11.

quick capacity to distinguish the significant from the trivial or irrelevant.

As Eleanor Elliott writes in the article previously cited, "As one safeguard against mistakes, a trustee should make sure that he or she is with a first-class group."

Education of Trustees

Some men and women seem to be born trustees. Some have trusteeship thrust upon them. The majority, however, achieve trusteeship in the full sense of the term by dint of working at the job and by getting educated to their duties. In this respect they are no different from the trustees of colleges and universities or the directors of hospitals and museums. Trustees need to understand, as we have seen, what their organization is all about, what it is trying to do, what are the terms of its charter, what are the limitations on program, how they relate to professional staff or how the program can be managed if there is no staff, the nature of their fiscal responsibility, the obligation of public accountability, and so on.

Conventional wisdom holds that trustees educate themselves, chiefly by attending meetings and listening to their seniors on the board. This is important, but wasteful of time and talent. Full participation by new board members can be expedited if the chairperson and/or the CEO sit down with the new trustee and review the many facets of the board's operations briefly summarized above. Or this briefing can be accepted by the nominating committee as the culminating stage of its responsibilities. Sometimes new trustees will be parceled out among senior board members, who will answer questions and provide guidance for the first few meetings.

Education can occur in many settings. Conversation about foundation issues and problems before, after, and in between meetings can be very helpful. New trustees will find formal "indoctrination" sessions a quick way of getting up to speed. Some executive officers prepare a packet of background materials and working papers for new members. An increasingly useful device is the special board meeting devoted entirely to a broad review of foundation policies, assessment of successes and failures, and survey of new needs and opportunities. This can be a regularly scheduled board meeting, but one at which official business will not be conducted, or a special meeting in the form of a retreat where the setting and time allow more relaxed discussion.

A network of outside opportunities for trustee development has grown up in recent years, including programs by the Council on Foundations, regional associations of grantmakers, and affinity groups of grantmakers. The Council's *Foundation News, Newsletter,* and other publications provide useful information for trustees, and its Self-Study Program is an excellent device for making a thoughtful appraisal of board operations. As foundations learn to work together, their boards can see how others function. Trusteeship is a responsible business.

Length of Term

Foundation charters and bylaws can be delightfully vague about length of terms. In some foundations trustees are elected for life; in others, on an annual basis; in a third group, terms may be set for a given number of years. In the *1988 Foundation Management Report* by the Council on Foundations, 43 percent of private and 96 percent of community foundations have specified terms for trustee service with the percentage decreasing among private foundations from 60 percent to 30 percent, as one moves from large to small in size of assets.[6] Terms range from one year to nine years. Eighty-three percent of private foundations reported terms of three years or less, whereas 97 percent of community foundations indicated terms of three to five years.

Where terms are for one year, reelection is usually automatic— so automatic in fact that the formality of reelection is occasionally dispensed with or overlooked. The practice of electing trustees for specific terms (i.e., three, five, or seven years) has much in its favor, as it is possible to stagger the terms of trustees. This calls attention to the need for reelection and encourages the kind of planning so important for board membership.

---

[6] It is hard to say how typical these percentages are. They differ slightly from previous surveys, all of which are based on returns to the Council's questionnaire of its own membership (heavily tilted toward the larger foundations). What they do indicate is the range of current practice.

Succession and Renewal

All foundation boards face the problem of continuity and change, the one as essential as the other. Some plan of succession in board membership is therefore essential. Most charters or founding instruments do make some provision for this, but the provision is not self-operative or self-realizing. All too often, particularly among small family foundations, no serious thought is given to future board membership. Is it a reluctance on the part of elderly trustees to contemplate the possibility of death, the same reluctance that inhibits so many people from drawing up wills? Is it merely procrastination that seems to overtake us as we grow older and less vigorous? Whatever the reason, the result is unfortunate. Common sense suggests that some staggering of ages is desirable, so that all trustees will not reach the end of the road at the same time. And if family or other members have been designated to take over, it would be helpful to break them in under the guidance of senior trustees rather than to expect them to land running when death throws them onto a board.

Foundations, like people, grow old and become static. They need renewal. What has been called "the iron law of oligarchy" takes over.[7] Those with the greatest interest, energy, or ambition collect power around themselves and consciously or unconsciously push aside the contributions of others, especially if they are not supportive of the dominant group's program. It is easier to continue doing what one has done than to introduce change. Institutional renewal, say Manser and Cass, "is potentially a painful process—for someone. It is difficult to explain to a small group of dedicated board members that the program which they have served selflessly for many years must be phased out to give way to new methods of service."

There are two useful devices for facilitating renewal and change. One is to set an arbitrary retirement age. Many foundations do

---

[7] Manser and Cass: *Voluntarism at the Crossroads*, Family Service Association of America, New York, 1976, excerpted in *Philanthropy Monthly*, March 1976, pp. 27–28.

this; the majority do not. For Ford Foundation trustees, the retirement age is 70; for Rockefeller trustees, it is 65. During most of its history, the Carnegie Corporation had no mandatory retirement age, with the result that in earlier years some trustees served until past 80 and one past 90. In 1971 the age limit was set at 70, which seems to be the average for foundations with age restrictions. We all know individuals of 75 who have a more youthful outlook than their grandchildren, and one should not forget the bitter epitaph, "Died at 30, Buried at 60." Some cut-off point, hopefully this side of senility, would be an advantage to every board.

The second device is a mandatory limitation on the number of consecutive terms or years of service. It is less common than a fixed age of retirement and faces more resistance, perhaps because it is the more effective of the two in bringing about change. Where this principle is in effect, two or three successive terms constitute the normal pattern.

There are two great advantages to limiting the years of consecutive board service. First, it provides a graceful way of saying goodbye to a member who has outlived his or her usefulness. It avoids the embarrassment of explaining to a devoted board member why he or she is not being continued as a trustee. With termination dictated by the bylaws and therefore applying to everyone, no one can feel aggrieved. Second, it provides greater freedom to experiment with younger and different trustees. The board will not be stuck with them for life. In this way new faces, new viewpoints, and new sources of ideas can be tried on for size and discarded if not suitable.

Under this arrangement it is always possible to reelect to the board after the lapse of a year a former trustee whose services are invaluable. Presumably this will be an infrequent occurrence, so that no one will have reason to expect it or be hurt if it does not happen. It could be invoked for family members where family connection is deemed important. Or exceptions to these restrictions could be specified in the bylaws for family members, although the creation of a two-class system of trustees leaves much to be desired. Exception should, of course, be made for the chief executive officer of the foundation if he or she also serves as a trustee—a practice that appears to find increasing favor.[8]

Both continuity and change can be easily managed within the foundation by a little intelligent foresight and planning. The wise donor establishing a foundation during his or her life will write in certain restrictions respecting age and length of service—restrictions to which he or she might himself be an exception. The instrument establishing a foundation by bequest could easily do the same. Exceptions might be made for certain family members, but in time this becomes awkward and embarrassing. It would be much cleaner and simpler to recognize from the start the desirability of providing for constant renewal. For foundations now in existence, the trustees have it in their power to add or amend bylaws that would accomplish this purpose. It is a simple change with significant consequences.[9]

---

[8] The Julius Rosenwald Fund limited trustee service to two successive three-year terms (permitting reelection if desirable after the lapse of one year), but made exceptions for the chairman, Mr. Rosenwald, and the president, who was the chief executive officer. The bylaws of the Southern Education Foundation permit trustees to serve two successive four-year terms and after a lapse of at least one year a third four-year term (but no more). Former trustees may be appointed to an Advisory Board "to provide continuing advice to the Board of Trustees in managing the affairs of the Corporation."

[9] The committee of inquiry set up by the National Council of Social Service in England, under the chairmanship of Lord Goodwin, examined these questions. In its report, *Charity Law and Voluntary Organizations*, 1976, the committee concluded: "We recommend (a) that all charities should normally have in their trust instrument a provision for rotation of trustees other than ex officio trustees; (b) that there should be an age limit of 70 for trustees other than ex officio trustees; (c) that these provisions should apply immediately to new trustees and to existing trustees after three years. . . ." Rotation of membership is fast becoming the standard practice on college and university boards.

CHAPTER 7

The Dynamics of an Effective Board

Since ultimate responsibility rests with the trustees, it is of the utmost importance that they become an effective governing body, fully acquainted with the purposes, the past accomplishments, and the potentialities of the organization they direct.

F. EMERSON ANDREWS

Most foundations, large or small, seem not to spend much time in thinking about organization. Such questions, however, need to be raised from time to time: Officers? Bylaws? Board committees? Board-and-staff committees? Rigidity or flexibility? How much of each?

MERRIMON CUNINGGIM

The observation that the whole is greater than the sum of its parts is true of most social organizations, including governing boards. In the two preceding chapters, the importance of the qualities of individual board members has been emphasized as well as the value of a mix of diverse qualities. The effective functioning of a foundation board, however, will also depend on the organization and leadership of the board. These practical considerations belong to what the social scientists call group dynamics.[1]

Size

It is a common adage that individual responsibility varies inversely with the size of the board. The smaller the board, the greater is

---

[1] I am particularly indebted in this chapter to a review of the findings of the social scientists on group dynamics by Sally Miller Watson.

likely to be the feeling of unity, of common purpose, of involvement, of participation in the board's decisions, of responsibility for the organization. The larger the board, on the other hand, the greater the range of viewpoints and ideas, and the more balanced and judicious the final consensus is likely to be. Foundations, unlike colleges, orchestras, museums, et al., do not have to raise money to meet annual budgets (although community foundations must seek added capital funds); nor do they operate complex public programs involving people experienced in public and community relations, such as the Red Cross, the Girl Scouts, and a host of others. Therefore, they do not need the large board characteristic of educational, cultural, and service institutions.

We noted in chapter 5 that the average size of foundation boards depends on the sample surveyed. In general, community foundation boards, for reasons stated above, tend to run larger; company-sponsored foundation boards, smaller. The big independent foundations, with their wide-ranging responsibilities and need to divide up the workload, tend toward large boards. Small and especially family foundations can manage with fewer trustees. But there are many exceptions. Most founding instruments allow a certain leeway, and, as time goes on, boards must decide on the basis of experience the ideal size for each one.[2]

---

[2] Some foundations have a single trust company as trustee. Small family foundations often have three-to-five member boards. The Ford Foundation has nineteen, Carnegie seventeen, Rockefeller and Robert Wood Johnson Foundations sixteen each, while the Lilly Endowment has only seven. In 1972 the District Court of Galveston, Texas, ordered an increase in the board of the Moody Foundation from three as specified in the indenture creating the foundation to seven. "After considerable reflection and study in the matter," wrote Judge Godard, "I have concluded that due to the size, function and complexity of the Foundation and for the orderly and efficient operation of same, the Board of Trustees should be expanded so that it could better cope with the demands of today and the future." On appeal, the lower court was reversed, and the Foundation, with assets over $200 million has continued to be governed by three family trustees, one of whom was recently removed by court order for defrauding the foundation.

Frequency of Meetings

The following table is based on information provided by 505 members of the Council on Foundations for its *1986 Foundation Management Report:*

| | Percent | | |
| | Private | Community | |
Meeting Frequency	Foundations	Foundations	Total
1 per year	8	4	7
2 per year	15	5	12
3 per year	17	8	15
4 per year	34	33	34
5–10 per year	20	34	24
Over 10 per year	6	16	9

Forty percent of the private foundations meet three times per year or less, whereas 83 percent of the community foundations meet four times per year or more.[3] In 1969 the Peterson Commission, using a smaller stratified sample of foundations, found 9 percent that never met, less than 0.5 percent that met every few years, and 11 percent that met whenever necessary.

The larger and more varied the foundation program, the greater is the need for frequent meetings. Small family foundations find less need for formal meetings since decisions can often be reached through informal family communication. The practice of having no board meetings, however, is a dubious procedure, and, when minutes are written up as though there had been meetings, it borders on evasion of legal responsibilities.[4]

---

[3] The members of the distribution committee of the Cleveland Foundation meet four times per year plus an annual meeting and serve on several sub-committees, each of which meets four or five times per year. As a result, each member attends between 15–17 meetings per year.

[4] Note the following comments from the *Proceedings of the 7th Biennial Conference on Charitable Foundations,* New York University, 1965: "Full and accurate minutes of foundation meetings are a necessity from a legal, tax status and practical standpoint. Needless to add, it is important to have a consistently good attendance of trustees or directors to obtain the benefit of full and varied discussions. Trustees or directors who are absent from a meeting should promptly be sent complete copies of the minutes. However, it is emphasized that there is no substitute for personal discussion on foundation matters. 'Conference calls,' resumes, etc., cannot possibly serve as a substitute for a face-to-face meeting at which all problems are fully discussed" (pp. 104–105).

Unless an executive committee, meeting frequently, takes over the responsibilities of the full board or unless the board hands over its responsibilities for major decisions to the staff, it is difficult to see how only yearly meetings can be justified, and there are serious objections to both conditions. Semi-annual meetings are the minimum necessary for even special interest foundations. Three to five meetings per year would seem to be desirable, depending on the breadth of program interests and the funds available for grants. Operating foundations have different needs, determined by whether the trustees merely set the course and review the operations of staff or whether they themselves become involved in the program.

Length of Meetings

With respect to length of board meetings, the *1986 Foundation Management Report* (based on a disproportionate number of large and staffed foundations) gives us the following information:

	Percent*		
Length of Meeting	Private Foundations	Community Foundations	Total
1 Hour	6	6	6
2 Hours	26	55	34
3 Hours	24	21	23
4 Hours	19	10	17
5–10 Hours	19	7	16
Over 10 Hours	5	1	4

* This table does not include corporate foundations or giving programs.

It is interesting to note that whereas 40 percent of private foundations meet three times per year or less, 43 percent hold meetings lasting four hours or longer. Almost the same percent of community foundations that meet four or more times per year hold meetings that last three hours or less, 55 percent being two hours long. Length and frequency of meetings clearly tend to vary inversely.

Here again the Peterson Commission found startling comparisons. According to its sample, 14 percent of foundations hold meetings lasting no longer than 15 minutes; 11 percent, meetings of 15–30 minutes; and 16 percent, meetings between 30 minutes and one hour. These represent less than 10 percent of foundation assets. In contrast, the trustees of the Ford Foundation meet four times a year for two and a half days (Tuesday morning through Thursday lunch with dinner meetings on Tuesday and Wednesday). With travel time for those living away from New York, this amounts to four weekdays four times a year plus committee service and considerable homework—a not inconsiderable commitment for busy people.

The length of board meetings ought to depend on the amount of business to be done and will depend on the degree of trustee involvement in the foundation's affairs. The trustees of one major foundation with assets in excess of $200 million meet three times per year for one and a half to two hours per meeting, chiefly to ratify staff recommendations. One small foundation with grants around $350,000 holds two meetings per year extended over an afternoon, evening, and the following morning. The trustees, presented by staff with worthwhile proposals in excess of available funds, engage in lively and prolonged discussion before deciding which proposals to support. Some decisions, especially where important issues of policy are involved, will need more time than others. Approval of a bank's or investment counselor's recommendations may take less time than direct management of the foundation's portfolio by the trustees themselves; but the board has the obligation, as we shall see in chapter 12, to set investment goals and to review investment strategies. To do this properly takes time.

Where trustees are readily available, as with most community foundations, frequent meetings can be easily scheduled. The danger, however, of frequent short meetings is concentration on investment decisions and specific grantmaking at the expense of proper consideration of long-range program and policy issues. Important problems need to be talked out at length. Important decisions should not be made under pressure of time. Each board must find the best balance for its purposes.

Organization

How much structure or articulation should a foundation have? Whatever is necessary for the most effective operation is the answer. Most foundations are corporations. As corporations, they require bylaws, which, among other things, provide for the election of officers and the appointment of standing and ad hoc committees.

Small family foundations need a minimum of committee structure. The demands of investment, grantmaking, and control are modest enough to permit their satisfaction by the board as a whole. Many foundations without staff would find it helpful to set up program and evaluation committees to divide up the work and to ease the burden on the entire board. For middle- and large-sized foundations, however, effectiveness will depend in no small part on the organization of the board. Most of these foundations have an executive committee, a finance committee, one or more program committees, and sometimes committees on audit, personnel, evaluation, and the like. As argued in the preceding chapter, the nominating committee is a very important one, preferably as a standing committee, but at least on an ad hoc basis. Ad hoc committees for the selection of a new CEO, for a move to a new location, for an analysis and evaluation of foundation performance, and for many other purposes will prevent the overloading of standing committees. Committee structure, however, can occasionally become so elaborate that it defeats its purpose of providing greater efficiency and of saving the time and energy of the board.

The executive committee is the most important one, since it exercises all or most of the powers of the board. Small in number, it normally consists of senior or prominent or more accessible trustees. It meets on call or on a regular—usually monthly—schedule between board meetings. It can easily become a powerful, indeed dominating, group within the board, an inner circle as it were, with the unfortunate result that other trustees come to see themselves as second-class citizens and lose interest. It was this concern that led the trustees of the Carnegie Corporation in their 1971 reorganization to abolish the executive committee entirely.[5] Nevertheless, for foundations with only two or three meetings per year, an executive committee is almost indispensable. Emergencies demand quick action. Some grant requests cannot wait for the next scheduled board meeting. The executive committee provides an element of flexibility. But it must remember that it is the servant, not the master, of the board.

The creation of one or more program committees depends upon the extent to which the trustees wish to become involved in actual grantmaking. In small family foundations, with or without staff, this is normally viewed as a responsibility of the trustees as a whole. In other foundations, some boards are prepared to leave individual grant decisions to the staff with pro forma board approval; some accept the recommendations of a program committee that has worked its way through the thicket of grant requests; some assign trustees to one of several program committees, each dealing with one major aspect of the foundation's total program.

Budget, finance, investment, administrative, and similar committees exist to facilitate the necessary housekeeping that is a part of all organizational activity.

The Chairperson's Role

Of all the trustees, the chairperson plays front and center. By personal example, by persuasion, or, if necessary, by coercion, he or she must lead the other trustees in fulfilling their responsibilities. The chairperson is the trustee to whom staff should turn when problems arise as well as being the board member primarily

---

[5] Note Haskins' comments in the article cited previously: "With a lowered quorum for a meeting of the full board, the placement of nominations in the hands of a new committee for this purpose, and the addition of some administrative responsibilities to those of finance and investment in a revamped committee, it was decided, as indicated earlier, to dispense with an executive committee. In some organizations an executive committee may, over a period of time, become the 'in' group of the board, with a corresponding loss of interest and attention of other trustees. We wished to guard against this, particularly in the light of other recommendations to have more trustees from a wider geographical area and our special concern that the full board be fully and actively involved in the selection and review of the broad substantive programs of the Corporation" (p. 12).

concerned with staff performance and staff well-being. His or hers is the responsibility to make certain that a trustee with special professional competence or experience does not become a self-appointed expert, limiting the foundation to his or her particular judgments. Trustee skills and knowledge need to be used, but individual trustees should not be allowed to dominate the board's decision by claims to knowledge not revealed to other trustees. In short, the chairperson must be prepared to give more time and thought to the affairs of the foundation than other trustees.

One word of caution is worth remembering in this connection. The very qualities of leadership and statesmanship so important for the chairperson can degenerate in time into dictatorship. Occasionally a chairperson, just because of deep concern and involvement, may assume too much authority, and the board can become a one-man show. The simplest way to guard against this danger, and a good practice even where the danger is believed not to exist, is to limit the chairperson's term of office. The Carnegie Corporation, e.g., has made it five years. Whatever the term, it will be tempting to extend the tenure of a good chairperson for all the obvious reasons of devotion, time, prestige, ability, and the like. One buys current ease at the price of future trouble.

The Role of the CEO

For foundations with professional staff, the role of the top administrator is one more factor influencing board performance. The selection of the chief operating officer is the responsibility of the trustees; many would say it is their most important responsibility. It is the duty of the executive director or president to carry out the program and policies approved by the trustees. The reputation of the foundation will depend in part on how well he or she fulfills that task.

Some executive directors, particularly in family-dominated foundations, are expected to carry out orders. Others are authorized to investigate and report on grant opportunities in which the board is interested. An increasing number of directors consists of professionally trained individuals who bring wide background knowledge, initiative, and independent judgment to help shape the thinking of the board. The presence of staff of this stature and their interaction with trustees profoundly affect board performance. This relation is so important that it will be further developed in the following two chapters. Suffice it to note here that it must be a relation of mutual trust and confidence if the board is to perform at its best.

The Agenda

What a board decides—read: how a board performs—depends on what it has to act on, i.e., the agenda. Who sets the agenda—the chairperson, the CEO, the vocal dissident, or some combination of the above? Is the agenda planned ahead, written out, distributed well in advance of the meeting, or does it spring like Juno fully formed from the the brow of the chairperson?

Two dangers threaten the agenda. It can become so casual and haphazard as to give no real direction and movement to the board's deliberations. Decisions do get made, but by accident rather than by design, and they run a high risk of being incorrect. Or the agenda can become so rigid that there is no room for the really significant issues or for adequate consideration of unanticipated situations. Some bylaws prescribe in detail the order of business. Some boards, impatient to complete all necessary business by the promised adjournment time, will concentrate on investment decisions or on approving specific grants and leave no time for larger problems.

Agendas are made for boards, not boards for agendas. Wisely planned in advance, they facilitate the work of the board. This planning is the responsibility of the chairperson in unstaffed foundations and the chairperson together with the chief staff officer in staffed foundations. Some housekeeping business—bank signature authorizations, rental contracts, salary adjustments, etc.—must be disposed of, but it should be done quickly. Reports of officers and committees should be circulated in advance, not read at the meeting, and the authors should be prepared to answer questions.

The important issues should be put front and center, and they should be presented in a way that invites discussion—the issue succinctly stated, the possible choices, the arguments (briefly) for each choice including the probable consequences. All this should be presented in advance of the meeting. Board meetings should never be dull.

Physical Setting

The atmosphere in which board discussion takes place can have a subtle but significant effect on the outcome. Should board meetings be relaxed and informal, or should they be strictly business-like? Too much informality may create the impression that the board's business is not very important. Conversely, highly structured, let's-not-waste-any-time procedures can inhibit discussion, dull the interest, and destroy the satisfaction of the participants. Many foundations solve the problem by combining lunch with an afternoon meeting, dinner with an evening meeting, or some similar combination. Others vary the place of meeting, scheduling periodic "retreats" for policy issues or general discussion in more relaxed locations than the conventional board room. This encourages leisurely and free-wheeling discussion.

Even such little things as the shape of the table and the arrangement of chairs make a difference. A classroom setting with the chairperson (like a teacher) up front is not conducive to the best discussion. Trustees should sit at tables where they can spread out their papers, and the tables should be arranged (hollow square or rectangle) so that every trustee can see and hear every other trustee. Uncomfortable chairs make people restless; overstuffed chairs tend to make them sleepy. All this is obvious—and often ignored.

Group Morale

Nothing is so contagious as enthusiasm. In addition to all the other factors affecting a board's performance, there is the sense of common purpose, of a shared enterprise, the pleasure in serving the welfare of mankind, the satisfaction of a job well done. Board meetings should be exciting. If time permits, outside experts might open up to new vistas or challenge traditional foundation assumptions; audio-visual evidence of successful programs enjoying foundation support might be shown. Board meetings should be so staged as to bring out new, interesting, and exciting ideas.

All this presupposes that trustees are fulfilling their proper responsibilities, i.e., to do their homework, to attend meetings, and to take an active part in the decisions. If everyone does his or her part, board meetings will be looked forward to with anticipation and looked back on with the realization that one's horizons have been expanded by the experience. Morale is an elusive quality. When trustees as a group have it, they know it, and they work more effectively for a common cause.

CHAPTER 8

To Staff or Not To Staff

Trusteeship requires a prejudice against avoidable waste or unnecessary costs of overhead and administration . . . And although I suspect that this sensitivity can be easily and unduly exaggerated, it is a sound instinct and one to which endowed philanthropy should pay close attention.

DEAN RUSK

The vast majority of U.S. foundations currently function without executive leadership, and hence philanthropy, using the words of Santayana, "rushes down any untrodden path it finds alluring." . . . I believe that the rapid development of a cadre of foundation executives capable of advancing the enlightened interests of foundations is a matter of organizational survival.

ROBERT W. BONINE

And the very question of whether philanthropy can or should be a career or a profession is arguable. The job market is minuscule; appointments are idiosyncratic; lateral and upward mobility is limited; skill comes mostly from experience, and experience is not widely accepted as transferable; and even the professionals wonder if long service in philanthropy is good for them or society.

PAUL YLVISAKER

"Somebody must sweat blood with gift money if its effect is not to do more harm than good," wrote Henry S. Pritchett, president of the Carnegie Corporation, many years ago.[1] That "somebody"

[1] *Annual Report,* 1922, p. 12.

must be either the trustees or the staff, and since an enormous amount of hard work is involved, it is surprising that so few boards make use of professional staff. In a nation that has elevated business management to a high art, the paucity of comparable management in the philanthropic world is the more conspicuous.

The Staffing Picture

The earliest study of foundation staffing is to be found in *The Foundation Administrator* by Arnold J. Zurcher and Jane Dustan.[2] Using elaborate investigating techniques, the authors could discover in 1970–1971 only 212 foundations employing one or more full-time professional staff and 343 employing full-time or part-time professionals. Of the 1,062 full-time staff, Ford employed 25 percent; Rockefeller, 15 percent; and eleven other large foundations, 12 percent. In short, thirteen foundations employed 52 percent of professional staff. One would not expect to find many professional staff among the small family foundations composing the great bulk of the foundation world. What was surprising was that 159 foundations with assets of $1–10 million and 133 foundations with assets ranging from $10 million to $1 billion operated without any professional staff.

The situation has significantly changed since the Zurcher and Dustan study. The technical requirements of the 1969 Tax Reform Act have induced many foundations to employ clerical help, either full-time or part-time. Common sense has led many boards to recognize the importance of staff in providing greater accessibility, better reporting, and more careful programming.

The most recent figures come from the Council on Foundations' *1988 Foundation Management Report*. According to its survey of its members and members of some regional associations, 79 percent had some staff, professional or supporting or both. The number of staff ranged from zero to 43 for community foundations and

---

[2] Russell Sage Foundation, 1972. Zurcher was for many years on the staff of the Alfred P. Sloan Foundation. Jane Dustan is vice president of the Foundation for Child Development. Although the statistics are now out of date, this is a thoughtful examination of the role and the problems of foundation staff. See also Zurcher, *The Management of American Foundations*, New York University Press, 1972.

to 330 for independent foundations, the median being four for community and four for independent foundations (three full-time, one part-time). It must be remembered that Council membership is heavily tilted toward the larger and staffed foundations. The best current estimate is that fewer than seven percent of foundations have staff and that the entire foundation field employs around 8,000 full- and part-time staff.[3] This is a lot better than the 1970–1971 figures. But is it good enough?

Disadvantages of Staff

Three arguments are offered for not employing staff or for keeping staff to a minimum.

The first and most obvious is cost. A large foundation making annual grants in the millions can afford a large staff; a small foundation with grants in the thousands cannot. There needs to be some sensible relationship between the sum total of grants awarded or programs underwritten and the cost of carrying on business.[4]

A second potential disadvantage of staffed foundations is lack of flexibility. "A key staff appointment," writes former Rockefeller Foundation President Dean Rusk in the article from which the

---

[3] See Deborah Brody, "More Than a Salary Survey," in *Foundation News*, September/October 1987, pp. 61–62. (The Foundation Center also conducts a staff survey. The most recent results are reported in the 11th Edition of *The Foundation Directory*.)

[4] Consider the advice of Carl Gerstacker, trustee of two foundations, each with assets between $20 and $30 million: "My recommendation, therefore, is for discipline. Government never knows when to stop expanding its services; it has no marketplace to tell it that it has gone too far, as business has. In the same way, foundations often don't know how much to spend on administration. The problem is always where to stop. So keep your administrative expenses and staff to the bare-bones minimum." "Let 'Outsiders' Control Family Foundation Boards," in *Foundation News*, September/October 1975, p. 18.

The charge that some foundations allowed excessive overhead expenses was one of the reasons for restrictions in the 1969 Tax Reform Act. The Deficit Reduction Act 1984 further specified that not more than 0.65 percent of a foundation's assets (averaged over three years) could be applied to meeting the payout requirement of five percent of assets. In other words, while larger expenditures for administration are legitimate if "reasonable and necessary," expenditures above 0.65 percent of assets will not count toward the payout requirement.

opening quotation was taken, "usually turns out to be a program decision, because a key staff appointment tends to set the framework of experience, intelligence, and imagination within which questions will be considered at staff level." This creates no problem so long as the area of staff competence coincides with the foundation's major program, but it has been known to restrict the freedom of the foundation to change its program.

And finally there is the danger that staff, particularly where there is a large staff, will take over from the trustees and for all practical purposes run the foundation according to their own ideas, which may not always be consistent with the donor's intent. This is one of the concerns of the recently articulate "conservative" foundations.[5] Quite apart from the political aspect, however, staff direction is both useful and desirable, particularly in middle- and large-sized foundations. But it should occur within a setting where it is clear to all concerned that the trustees have the final decision. This has not always been the case.

Advantages of Staff

Staff provides three major advantages to foundations. The first is efficiency. A lot of work is involved in all but the smallest foundations—more work than most trustees are prepared or should be expected to undertake. Financial records must be kept. Reporting forms must be filed. Requests for information should be answered. Requests for grants need to be investigated, and grants once made should be followed up. With competing needs in terms of the public good (environment versus prison reform, education versus aid to the homeless) and grant requests in excess of available funds, pregrant evaluation is essential to intelligent grantmaking. And postgrant evaluation, more honored in the breach than the observance, is the only way to learn from one's successes

---

[5] Consider the comment by Leslie Lenkowsky, president of the Institute for Educational Affairs (described as "the conservative interest group in the philanthropic world") in an interview with *The Chronicle of Higher Education,* September 2, 1987: "Well, if in fact the dominant view in the field is that philanthropy is a kind of change agent, where ultimate virtue is to be found in creating a new government program, that's not going to rub off very well on the kind of people who are capable of setting up foundations" (p. A75).

and mistakes. To economize on staff may turn out to be penny wise and pound foolish. A low-cost grant ill thought out or inadequately investigated may prove to be a high-cost waste of foundation money. The need for staff will vary with the size and nature of the foundation. The larger and more general the purposes, the greater the need for professional help; but all *Foundation Directory*-size foundations, save those with trustees who virtually make a career of managing them, would improve their efficiency with administrative assistance. Too many that could well afford such help are limping along without it.

A second major purpose served by staff is accountability, and in this context, visibility and communication are twin aspects of accountability. Too many foundations are tucked away out of sight, and access to them is deliberately made difficult. Too many foundations fail to answer their mail. It is difficult to communicate with a post office box that does not respond. This privacy, as we have seen, is the basis for much criticism of foundations. Responding to requests for help is not only a matter of courtesy; it is a moral obligation. It is hard for trustees, for whom board service is viewed as family loyalty or *pro bono publico* activity, to fulfill this obligation. This is an important function of staff.

The third advantage is the contribution that staff can and do make to the agencies supported by the foundation and to many of those whose requests are declined. The personal concern and professional help of staff will often be more valuable than the grant itself. While care must be observed not to interfere with or dictate to requesting organizations, many need help with their internal operations or their proposed budgets. Some need assistance in rewriting their proposals. Others need guidance on where to turn for support. Staff members of the larger community foundations are making important contributions in these ways, but even small family foundations, such as the Dyer-Ives Foundation in Grand Rapids, Michigan, are often more helpful with their advice and assistance than with their limited grants.

Shared Staff

Small foundations cannot afford full-time staff. The cost would be clearly disproportionate. Many, however, can afford part-time employees, who are shared with the family business, with corporations in company-sponsored foundations, or with other foundations. It is not uncommon for the same corporate officers to manage the corporation's foundation and also its direct-giving program. It is becoming increasingly common for foundations to share staff with one another. Among the respondents in the *1988 Foundation Management Report,* 31 percent indicated some form of sharing.

Two examples will illustrate this point: (1) Joint Foundation Support was established in 1968 in New York City "by a group of small foundations with similar interests and a common need for administrative and research support." JFS does most of the preliminary investigation and assumes administrative responsibility for the grants. Each member decides what proposals to support. Currently there are thirteen members. (2) In 1986 nineteen unstaffed Philadelphia area foundations formed the Delaware Valley Network of Trustee Managed Foundations to exchange information and ideas about management problems, tax code issues, trends in philanthropy, annual reports, and the like. The members meet several times a year, but have no separate office or staff.

More and more community foundations are functioning as clearinghouses and service agencies for small unstaffed independent foundations. Typical of this service was the extensive study of community needs made by a special committee of the San Diego Community Foundation in 1985—a study that provided an overall context not only for their own grantmaking, but also for philanthropic support by other foundations, corporations, and government agencies in the area. Small unstaffed foundations are turning to community foundations for information and advice. In turn, community foundations can direct grantseekers to those sources most likely to give them sympathetic hearing. Even among the larger staffed foundations, cooperation has become much more common.

Consultants

Sixty-one percent of the foundations surveyed for the Council's *1988 Foundation Management Report* reported that they made use of consultants, chiefly in the areas of accounting, investment, and legal problems, but also for advice on programs, for investigation of prospective grantees, and for postgrant evaluations. Among large foundations, the use of experts on an ad hoc basis reduces the need for permanent staff and safeguards flexibility of program. Among small foundations with part-time or no staff, consultants can often serve the purpose of staff at lower cost. In both situations it is well to keep in mind the adage of former President Frederick Keppel of the Carnegie Corporation, who used to say that he would rather "buy his milk than keep a cow."[6]

Staff Profile

What we know about foundation employees is based on surveys of the approximately 1,100 members of the Council on Foundations plus some additional members of regional associations. Since Council members are among the larger and staffed foundations and since roughly only 50 percent responded to inquiries, the results may not characterize the foundation universe as a whole. On the other hand, the responses came from foundations employing slightly under 50 percent of the estimated 8,000 foundation employees and may, therefore, give a reasonably accurate picture of the employee world.[7]

Over half of foundation staff consists of professionals; slightly less are support staff. Professionals are those who participate in decisions about program areas and individual grants or have major administrative responsibilities. Support staff perform the accounting, bookkeeping, and secretarial work essential to any well-run office. Staff membership is 26 percent male, 74 percent female. Eighty-five percent are white, while 15 percent come from minority groups.

In the latest survey, 59 percent of the chief executive officers were male and the rest female—a substantial improvement in the status of women. Most of the women CEOs were in the smaller

---

[6] Quoted in F. Emerson Andrews' *Philanthropic Foundations*, p. 131.

[7] The figures in this section are taken from the *1988 Foundation Management Report*. See also Deborah Brody's "How Foundations Do It," in *Foundation News*, November/December 1988, pp. 61–62.

foundations. Turnover is fairly high with half the CEOs in their jobs five years or less and 19 percent two years or less. The average length of employment for all foundation staff is five years.

In 1985, Odendahl, Boris, and Daniels published an important study of the career patterns of men and women under the title *Working in Foundations*. They followed up a questionnaire with interviews with 60 individuals working in 42 foundations (27 CEOS, 23 program officers, 10 administrative assistants). Among other things, they found that 75 percent of foundation officers were recruited in contrast to 25 percent who applied. The gender difference was striking: 4 percent of the men applied, 43 percent of the women. Graduation from a prestige college or university, service on nonprofit boards, and acquaintance with foundation board members were important factors leading to foundation appointment.

In some special purpose foundations, it may be important for the CEO to be a specialist, and some of the major foundations with large staffs can afford to have specialists in different program areas in which the foundation is interested. Most foundations, however, have chosen generalists—men and women with broad educational backgrounds and experience. Don Price succinctly states the rationale: "The top staff should have a range of competence and interests at least as broad as the total possibilities that are before the foundation or it will not be able to present to the trustees for decision the broad alternatives that ought to guide the foundation in the development of its program, year after year."[8]

Foundation employment is on its way to becoming a profession, but it has not yet arrived. There is no clear set of requirements or of skills. There is no widely recognized training program, although Yale, Michigan, Case Western Reserve, and other institutions are beginning to provide graduate studies in philanthropy. There are no widely accepted standards or code of conduct. The "Principles and Practices for Effective Grantmaking," developed

---

[8] Don K. Price: "Problems of Organization and Administration," New York University Second Biennial Conference on Foundations, 1955, p. 209.

by the Council on Foundations and subscribed to by its members, comes closest, but it is a set of guidelines for foundations, not individuals. Philanthropists have no professional association comparable to the American Medical Association, the American Institute of Architects, or the American Society of Civil Engineers.[9]

There is no dearth of candidates, for plenty of people think it would be a pleasant occupation to give away other people's money. Good administrators, however, are no easier to find in the foundation field than in any other. Indeed, in some respects, they may be harder to find for the reasons pointed out by Ylvisaker in the quotation heading this chapter. The opportunities are tremendous. The occupational hazards are insidious—the growth of attitudes of omniscience, omnipotence, and arrogance. Alan Pifer, reflecting on 30 years of work at the Carnegie Corporation, offers a devastating account of what can happen.[10]

Board Responsibility for Staff

"The closer I come to the end [of my career]," writes the president of one of the major foundations, "the surer I am that the most difficult and important task of a board of trustees is the selection, and if necessary dismissal, of the president, chief executive officer."[11] In this respect, foundation boards have the same responsibility as the boards of colleges and universities. While the CEO has the responsibility for all additional staffing, he or she should operate within the framework of personnel policies established

---

[9] See Judith K. Healey's fine article, "Not Yet a Profession," in *Foundation News,* July/August 1987.

[10] *Speaking Out: Reflections on 30 Years of Foundation Work,* Council on Foundations, 1984. This short and pithy pamphlet is well worth reading in its entirety, but see especially the chapter entitled "The Conduct of Foundation Officers." "Staff members," writes Roy W. Menninger of the Menninger Foundation, "sometimes find it hard to remain properly humble when they believe they are probably brighter, and certainly wiser, than either the board or the seekers. Succumbing to the seductions of the God complex is a real occupational hazard. Having money to give away and the power to decide whom to give it to is intoxicating, and foundations can be irritating examples of the 'narcissism of the righteous.' " *Foundation Work May Be Hazardous to Your Mental Health,* Council on Foundations pamphlet 1981, p. 11.

[11] Letter to the author.

by the board. These policies should cover salaries, retirement plans, health benefits, vacation and sick leaves, opportunities for professional improvement, and the like. Leaves of absence, freedom for outside activities, encouragement to pursue one's professional career and writing—all these help to keep staff alive and growing and thereby improve the operations of the foundation.

In recent years the Council on Foundations has held five-day Institutes for New Staff. These cover the major problems that staff members are likely to encounter and review the many facets of grantmaking. Some regional associations are beginning to hold comparable programs for their own areas. The Southern California Association for Philanthropy, for example, stages a three-day program on the Fundamentals of Grantmaking with a certificate of achievement awarded for the completion of the course.

Such programs are helpful for new staff. Other Council programs provide aid and comfort to overworked chief administrators, but they do not solve their psychological hang-ups. The pressures of increasing requests, of constantly saying no to worthwhile proposals, or reconciling staff recommendations with trustee decisions lead to burnout. This is a growing phenomenon and one to which boards need to give attention.[12]

---

[12] See Joseph Foote: "Stretching the Career Ladder," in *Foundation News,* January/February 1985. See also Roy W. Menninger: op. cit, p. 12.

CHAPTER 9

The Management of Foundations: Respective Roles of Trustees and Staff

One must look to the bureaucratic organization of the foundation, the character of foundation personnel, the role of trustees, and the foundation's self-image to understand why foundations operate as they do. Simply reading their alleged 'programs' does not tell one very much.

STANLEY N. KATZ

The staff-board relationship is crucial to effective foundation operation. Successful foundation management requires good communication and a delicate balance of power between trustees and employees.

ODENDAHL, BORIS, AND DANIELS

This chapter is addressed primarily, but not exclusively, to staffed foundations. Good management is important for all foundations, but those with professional staff face special problems.

Who runs the foundation? In theory, the board controls and sets policy; the staff manages the day-to-day operations. In practice, however, the division of power between board and staff takes many forms. The resulting problem is not unique to foundations; it surfaces on college and university campuses, in hospital and museum board rooms, and even, although less frequently, in corporate headquarters. Perhaps because trustees have greater responsibilities for foundation management, the division of authority between board and staff is frequently a troublesome source of tension within foundations. Paul Ylvisaker writes:

> These tensions stem from differences among trustees in which staff can easily get caught; differences in personalities and perspectives; conflicting interpretations of board and staff prerogatives; the constant need for staff to deal reliably and authoritatively with applicants, and the imperative for trustees to reserve judgment; the inherent subjectivity in analyzing and deciding social issues; the impatience, particularly among younger staff, to "accomplish something" and the understandable conservatism of board members, many of whom "have seen it all before"; and intermittently the reverse: a board growing weary of former novelty that has become routine and pressuring staff to come up with something exciting.[1]

Let us look at a variety of management models.[2]

Donor Model

Here there is no conflict (a) because there is no staff or only part-time clerical staff and (b) because all decisions are made by the donor who looks upon the foundation as an extension of his or her personal giving. The board may or may not discuss program and grants, but it is understood by all that the donor decides what the foundation will do.

Administrator Model

Many family foundations with limited assets and limited staff adopt this model. The board makes all the decisions. An administrator or office manager manages the office; handles inquiries by mail, telephone, or in person; collects information on grant

---

[1] "Foundations and Nonprofit Organizations," chapter 20 in *The Nonprofit Sector: A Research Handbook,* Yale University Press 1987, p. 364.

[2] I am indebted in this section to the excellent article by Teresa Odendahl and Elizabeth Boris, "A Delicate Balance: Foundation Board–Staff Relations," in *Foundations News,* May/June 1983. See also Odendahl, Boris, and Daniels, *Working in Foundations,* The Foundation Center 1985, p. 13.

requests; prepares material for board action; and carries out board decisions. There is no question of who controls the foundation, but tension and dissatisfaction will sometimes arise when the administrator is kept too long in a subordinate and routine position.

Director Model

Middle-sized foundations favor a management model, which puts an executive director (by whatever name) in the center of the stage, and some of the large foundations prefer this style. The board expects the executive director to help set the goals and shape the program of the foundation, to exercise his or her discretion in winnowing out unsatisfactory requests and in preparing a docket for board action. All decisions are jointly discussed in collegial fashion, often including program associates. The executive director may or may not be a voting member of the board, but he or she is clearly an active participant in board decisions about programs and grants. As board confidence in the executive director grows, he or she gains in stature and authority and becomes a persuasive, although not dominant, voice in the foundation's affairs.

Presidential Model

Most large foundations follow a pattern of strong central leadership. Odendahl, Boris, and Daniels describe it well in *Working in Foundations:*

> The presidential model is usually found in larger foundations that no longer have significant donor influence. Trustees delegate wide authority to the chief staff officer, who normally holds the title of president. The CEO provides leadership to foundation employees and the board. Trustees set fiscal and program policies, monitor progress, and make decisions on only very large grant proposals. Usually their CEO is someone nationally prominent, powerful, or well-respected in his own right. (p. 13).

The parallel to business practice is obvious. Indeed, Kenneth N. Dayton, former chairman of the Dayton Hudson Corporation and

member of many nonprofit boards, insists that there is no difference, save for the additional responsibility for volunteering services on the part of the nonprofit board member.[3] The danger of
course, is that a strong-minded CEO will take over the foundation
and the board will become window dressing.

Determination of Goals

The choice of model influences, if it does not dictate, the respective
roles of board and staff. This becomes evident in setting goals and
making grants.

Whatever else a board may or may not do, it is widely agreed
that it has the final responsibility, within the limits of the donor's
expressed requirements, of setting the foundation's policies and
goals. This is precisely what a board does when it periodically
sets aside time to review what its program has accomplished,
whether its money has been as well spent as it might have been,
and whether the foundation should tackle new problems in addition to or in place of old ones. This sometimes happens when
an individual trustee, exposed to a situation desperately in need
of help, is able to persuade his or her fellow trustees that the
foundation should take it on as its cause.

But this is not the way all foundations with professional staff
fashion their programs. In an illuminating chapter in *The Nonprofit Sector: A Research Handbook* already referred to, Melissa
Middleton questions the conventional view:

> Most of the data indicate that boards do not formulate policy but
> rather ratify policy that is presented to them by staff. The executive
> committee in concert with top management may be the only place
> within the board structure where policy is designed. Certain situa-
> tions (such as organizational transformations) may increase the
> likelihood that boards enact policy, but as a rule they do not.[4]

---

[3] Kenneth N. Dayton, "Define Your Roles," in *Foundation News*, May/June 1985.

[4] Chapter 8, "Nonprofit Boards of Directors: Beyond the Governance Function."
Middleton is discussing nonprofit organizations as a genus, of which foundations
are but one species. Nevertheless, her findings are relevant to the foundation
world.

Foundation boards hire competent professionals to run their foundations just as university boards hire presidents to run universities. In both cases, the trustees expect the professionals to have more expertise than they themselves possess. Should the foundation address third-world problems or the growing threat of AIDS? Whichever is chosen, what are the most promising strategies? Most boards would prefer to rely on full-time experts to study the problem and make recommendations.

Stanley Katz describes the relationship of board to staff as "a fascinating and complex problem":

> Suffice it to say that the principal problem seems to be how much scope foundation staff is to be given in the formulating and implementing of program. If the trustees are to maintain firm control of program, managers must be kept in reign (sic) and foundation programs will probably be quite stable and, very likely, conservative. The more freedom given to the managers, the greater opportunity for flexibility in working with a wide range of potential donees—and the greater the possibility that managers will be captured by the constituents they presumably seek to control. Most American foundations have tried to institutionalize some balance between these two states.[5]

Determination of Grants

The "fascinating and complex problem" exists in grantmaking as well as in setting programs. In the donor and administrator models, trustees decide on grants. In the director model, grant decisions are jointly arrived at. In the presidential model, the professional staff, and especially the CEO, will largely determine the grantmaking program within the areas already approved. The president of the Edward W. Hazen Foundation, for example, eliminates 90 percent of the requests for grants on her own authority. She presents at each board meeting proposals requesting twice the amount of money available, all of which in her judgment are worth funding. The trustees, who have received the docket in

---

[5] "Problems in Private Foundation Support of Academic Research: the United States Experience," 1981.

advance, then engage in a lively debate over which proposals to support. On the other hand, it has long been the practice of the trustees of the Carnegie Corporation (and many other large foundations) simply to approve the roster of grants presented by its president, albeit after lively discussion. To fulfill their responsibilities, trustees should at least review the requests turned down and feel free to raise questions.

Staff members work hard in shaping proposals for board action, and their work deserves understanding support. It can be frustrating and destructive of staff morale to develop a program of proposals in an area in which the board has evinced interest only to have them turned down in what appears to be arbitrary fashion. In working with some potential recipients, staff make implied commitments that become embarrassing if the board ignores them. Situations like these exacerbate the tensions between board and staff, sometimes resulting in an unfortunate attitude on the part of staff of "we" versus "them."

A balance of responsibilities between board and staff is needed but not always easy to achieve. In response to a question about the major responsibilities of foundation trustees, the president of a major and well-known American foundation replied:

> The single most urgent responsibility is to help the management
> of the foundation to find the right balance between sufficient in-
> volvement of trustees to get them well engaged in the foundation's
> business, on the one hand, and leaving the administration of the
> institution, and to a considerable extent the responsibility for pro-
> gram initiatives, in the hands of the foundation's chief executive
> and his/her staff.[6]

A workable balance will depend in large part on trust—trust in staff by board and respect for board by staff. With a new CEO and with new trustees, this will take time. Staff need to be sensitive to trustee interests and attitudes. A controversial proposal needs to be checked out with individual trustees in advance of full-

---

[6] Letter to the author.

board discussion. Trial balloons will reduce friction. We shall have more to say later on what generates trust on both sides.[7]

Evaluation

Good management requires evaluation of grantseekers, of the process by which grants are screened, of the results of grantmaking, of the staff who sort and recommend grants, and of the trustees who have the final responsibility.

Unless one is convinced of the merit of a requesting beneficiary, some pregrant investigation or inquiry is or should be standard operating procedure; to be so convinced that further appraisal is considered unnecessary presupposes prior knowledge and assessment. Pregrant evaluation may be thorough or perfunctory and may be conducted by staff or trustees or both. At whatever level, it is the basis on which grant decisions are made.

The process by which a request for support becomes an actual grant is as varied as foundations themselves. It is a process to which trustees need to give more and closer attention than most of them do. What happens to the inquiries that come by mail, telephone, or personal visit? Are they promptly and courteously answered? What kind of investigation is made? Who decides whether the proposal falls within the foundation's field of interest? What additional information is sought? Are trustees presented with more choices than they can fund? Does the CEO or the staff in conference select the proposals to be presented for board action? How are board decisions, whether positive or negative, reported to grantseekers? How long are supplicants kept waiting? These questions address the nuts and bolts of foun-

---

[7] Note, however, a less optimistic view at which Middleton arrives in the chapter cited above, bearing in mind that her data come from all types of nonprofit agencies. "The board-management relationship is essentially paradoxical. For many important decisions, the board is the final authority. Yet it must depend on the executive for most of its information and for policy articulation and implementation. The executive has these emergent powers but also is hired and can be fired by the board and needs the board for crucial external functions. As with all paradoxes, resolution is not possible. Instead the relationship is dynamic, and its movement depends on a number of individual, group, and organizational factors" (p. 152).

dation work. Trustees should demand efficient and courteous performance.

Foundations do not have profit and loss statements to tell them how well they are doing. Only a postgrant assessment of the results will reveal, to mix the metaphor, the foundation's hits, runs, and errors. This applies not only to individual grants, but also to program areas. Trustees should demand of someone— staff, consultants, or themselves if no one better—that they be given an honest account of what their grants have done. Have they pioneered in a new field or by new methods? Have they tossed money down a rat hole? Have they enabled a struggling organization to gain a real foothold? Have they merely lengthened the life of a moribund organization? Have grants been used for the purposes intended? Failures need to be studied as well as successes. A foundation without an occasional failure lacks either imagination or courage or both. The argument is offered that postgrant investigation is interference. This need not be the case. A more serious argument is offered that postgrant evaluation is expensive in time and money. It is. But uninformed grantmaking is more so.

The administrator, executive director, or CEO is hired by the board to run the foundation in accordance with the board's wishes and instructions. Any sensible employer will observe his or her employees to make certain that the latter are doing what they should. Thus, trustees must assess the performance of the chief executive officer and demand of the CEO that he or she evaluate subordinate staff. Foundation work, as noted in the last chapter, has its occupational hazards, and these need to be assessed in understanding fashion.

Trustees may, and in many foundations with competent staff they do, delegate responsibility for making grants up to some designated size or within some designated total amount; but in doing so they must decide those limits and establish procedures for reviewing what the chief administrator has done. McGeorge Bundy, former president of the Ford Foundation, lays down three principles determining the trustees' relation to the operating head:

> First, trustees should never keep a chief executive officer beyond the point when they are persuaded that they can do better with

someone else; second, trustees, even of very large, complex, and professionalized foundations, should not delegate even to the most trusted of presidents, their final responsibility for program choice; and third, even when—as they often should—they delegate wide direction in execution and give great weight to professional recommendations, trustees should make the fullest possible use, both formally and informally, of the power of constitutional monarchs elsewhere: to be informed, to advise, to warn—and I would add the quite different power to forbid.[8]

Finally, trustees need to evaluate their own performance. The governance of foundations is no easy matter. There are many management styles, as we have noted in this chapter, and in all of them the board of trustees has final responsibility. In light of recurrent criticisms from potential beneficiaries, from the general public, and from members of Congress, it is important that foundations be well governed—hence, the importance for governing boards of self-examination. This can be done with the help of the Council's *Self-Study Guide*, of an outside expert, of comparisons with comparable foundations, or of periodic sessions for self-analysis. The results, whatever the method, should be constructive. As Eugene Struckhoff has aptly said, the grantmaker is like the king who wore no clothes. No one will tell him, and he needs to know.

Board and Staff Obligations to Each Other

Much of this chapter has been an attempt to illuminate what Paul Ylvisaker calls "the almost inescapable tension between board and staff." It is important to emphasize, however, that some degree of tension is probably healthy, and the behavior of both board and staff can make it constructive rather than destructive.

In addition to carrying out their respective assignments, staff members need to keep trustees fully informed. They need to report changes both in character and in volume of requests for grants, their success in exploring new avenues of opportunity, and grant failures as well as grant successes. Trustees need to be educated on how foundation purposes might be met, on areas of growing

---

[8] "Foundation Trustees: Their Moral and Social Responsibilities," The Ford Foundation, 1975.

social or scientific or artistic need, and on the value of continuity of program versus the value of innovation. They should have information on administrative costs, on comparisons with comparable foundations, and with explanations of any significant differences. They should know what is happening in the foundation world, what new legal problems threaten, and what the critics have to say about foundation performance. Trustees must educate themselves; but where competent professional staff exists, it is one of the responsibilities of its members, and particularly of the CEO, to assist in the process. This is the "essentially paradoxical" relationship to which Middleton refers. The CEO is both agent and educator of the board, both employee and leader.

Conversely, the board has responsibilities toward the staff, as discussed in the preceding chapter. A wise board will also make certain that staff members feel involved in grantmaking decisions. Should the CEO be a member of the board? There is no hard and fast rule. Some CEOs feel it is important that they have trustee stature; others find it unimportant. Incidentally, the same ambivalence operates in college and university governance.

Should staff attend board meetings when program policies and grants are decided? Yes. The CEO should be present and participate. Program officers can make valuable contributions to board discussions and decisions as well. Some foundations have found it helpful to have all staff—support as well as professional—attend meetings, although this is the exception rather than the rule. Jing Lyman, trustee of several foundations, commented on her first meeting with the Enterprise Foundation, "It really pleased me that even the support staff were there. And everyone was introduced. . . . One of the important things that is overlooked in some foundations is a needed sense of community between the staff and the board."[9]

The Council's Principles and Practices

The wise management of foundations demands much thought, careful planning, and a basic commitment to the purposes for

---

[9] Quoted by Odendahl and Boris in their *Foundation News*, May/June 1983 article, "A Delicate Balance: Foundation Board–Staff Relations," p. 43.

which foundations exist. Over the past quarter century, the Council on Foundations has encouraged trustees and staff to share experiences and to develop acceptable patterns of performance. At the 1980 Annual Conference, members of the Council adopted an eleven-point statement of "Principles and Practices for Effective Grantmaking," and three years later they voted that acceptance of the statement in principle should be a condition of membership in the Council. The "Principles and Practices" are to be found on pages 147–149.

On Trustee–Staff Relationships

The following set of questions was drafted by Robert M. Johnson, when he was executive director of the Wieboldt Foundation in Chicago. It was printed in the September/October 1973 issue of *Foundation News* (p. 6).

Here's a Little Multiple Choice Quiz for You

What's a foundation staff's responsibility to its board with respect to grantmaking decisions? (Choose as many as you wish.)

1. To ask the board what it wants to give money to, and go out and find opportunities.
2. To be a channel through which pass applications—processing, distributing, sometimes researching, critiquing.
3. To screen applications and reduce their numbers to a more manageable few by helping the board at least identify some things it doesn't want to give money to.
4. To help board members (and staff) educate themselves about the realities of whatever fields they're interested in so they can make wiser decisions.
5. To help board members (and staff) educate themselves about the experiences of past grants and other foundations' grants so they'll be more sophisticated about philanthropy.
6. To become a leading thinker in the foundation's fields of interest because the board wants to take your word for it.
7. To become a leading thinker in your own fields of interest and get the board to agree to grants in them, one way or another.

8. To help board members, either individually or as a group, become more complete, aware people who will then be better philanthropists.
9. To help get other people to respect the foundation and its board.
10. To help board members rationalize their way into approving grants that are more (risky) (liberal) (countercultural) than they would approve if they knew what they were doing in the usual sense.
11. To help board members establish useful and fair rules for politicking among themselves on behalf of their respective favorite charities.
12. To help keep the board from getting into trouble with the IRS. ·
13. To help keep the board from getting into trouble with its friends, customers, etc.
14. To identify the board members who have the potential of being good philanthropists and work with them to develop their effectiveness on the board.

No matter how the choices sound, none are all good or all bad. I wager just as many philanthropic sins have been committed in the name of "helping board members educate themselves" as by trying to figure out which board members will agree with you and conspiring with them (no. 14). Within each option, there are acres and acres of fertile fields upon which the ancient foundation games between staff and board are played.

Try applying these alternatives to your own foundation, and remember that the ones you don't check can be just as revealing and useful to analyze as the ones you do check.

CHAPTER 10

Compensation of Trustees

Payment for the oversight of philanthropic activities is not in the American tradition. The trustees of educational institutions ranging from the public schools to universities and of health and welfare agencies traditionally receive no compensation. Yet the oversight of such institutions and agencies commonly requires more time and effort than does the management of a foundation, for the reason that a foundation is less likely to conduct an extensive operating program. However, it is in the American tradition to compensate trustees of trust funds, and this may have led to the payment of the trustees of a few foundations organized as trusts.

DONALD R. YOUNG

At a less fundamental level, but also troubling, is the growing tendency for trustees to pay themselves exorbitant fees for their part-time services. . . . This type of self-aggrandizement is not, happily, the general pattern, and there are many examples of dedicated, selfless performance by individual trustees. . . . But wherever it occurs it represents a deplorable perversion of the idea of voluntary service, and the practice now seems to be spreading.

WALDEMAR A. NIELSEN

No one knows how many foundations pay honoraria to their trustees. To find out, one would need to examine the 990-PF forms of the 25,639 foundations comprising the foundation world, and even such a search would not give a clear picture. A distinction needs to be made between honoraria or fees for services inherent in the nature of trusteeship and compensation for special services rendered as a result of the trustees' backgrounds

97

or professions in law, investment, real estate, or accounting. The information provided by the 990-PF forms does not make this distinction. Some of the figures in this chapter and elsewhere are rendered suspect by the confusion over what is included under compensation. The data in the Council on Foundations' surveys, however, are based on fees for service *as trustees*.

The best approximation we have for the number of foundations providing trustee honoraria comes from an unpublished survey in 1969 by F. Emerson Andrews. Using a five percent random sample, he reviewed the returns from 1,000 foundations, only 22 of which, or two percent, paid compensation for trustee service.[1] We do not know how accurate this percentage is. It is 20 years old, and, if Nielsen is correct, the number may today be higher. What we are reasonably sure of is that the trustees of the vast majority of foundations do not receive fees for their service as trustees.

On the other hand, we do have some information about the nature and extent of trustee compensation from the biennial reports of the Council on Foundations.

Council on Foundations 1988 Survey

Roughly 500 independent and private operating foundation members of the Council and of regional associations of grant-makers provided the following information about trustee compensation:

PERCENT OF FOUNDATIONS THAT DO (OR DO NOT) COMPENSATE TRUSTEES

	Percent				
Assets (mill's)	$100 and over (*n* = 67)	$25 to $99.9 (*n* = 87)	$10 to $24.9 (*n* = 65)	Under $10 (*n* = 161)	Total (*n* = 380)
All members compensated	35	26	18	28	107
Some members compensated	13	13	14	18	58
No members compensated	19	48	33	115	215

Respondents indicated by *n* (in parentheses) at head of each column.

---

[1] For what it is worth, the distribution of foundations by size in Andrews' sample corresponded very closely to the distribution by size among all foundations.

These figures must be used with caution, for the number of foundations involved is small, the response to the request for information was limited, and membership in the Council is heavily weighted toward the larger foundations. While, overall, 43 percent of the private foundations surveyed paid fees, 71 percent of those with assets of $100 million and over did so. No community foundations pay trustee fees, and few company-sponsored foundations do so.

There is no discernible pattern among those foundations that pay some, but not all, trustees. Some family foundations pay fees to nonfamily members, but not to the family; most company-sponsored foundations pay only outside directors. Some foundations pay the chairperson and/or other officers; some do just the reverse. Some pay a uniform honorarium to all trustees; some pay different amounts.

Type and Size of Fee

Among the 165 private foundations compensating trustees in the Council survey, the largest proportion (57 percent) paid an annual fee. Fifty-four percent paid fees per board meeting; 28 percent a fee per committee meeting; and 20 percent, some other fee. As might be expected, the large foundations with assets of $100 million or more had the highest percentages, with 85 percent paying annual fees to their board members and many of these paying fees per meeting as well. Compensation to trustees varies widely. In the Council's survey, summarized in the following table, the larger independent and operating foundations provided larger fees than the smaller foundations. Zurcher and Dustan, however, in their 1970–1971 study concluded "that compensation of trustees may rise to fairly generous levels—if there is any compensation at all—in foundations without staff and declines markedly as foundations take on staff."[2] This is understandable if compensation is based on management service as well as trustee service.

---

[2] Arnold J. Zurcher and Jane Dustan: *The Foundation Administrator*, Russell Sage Foundation, 1972, p. 101.

The following table gives data on private foundation fees from the 1988 Council survey:

TRUSTEE FEES

Assets (millions)	$100 and over	$25–$99.9	$10–$24.9	Under $10	Total
ANNUAL FEE					
Low	500	1,000	1,000	300	300
High	53,100	24,000	10,000	10,000	53,100
Median	10,000	6,000	4,000	2,400	5,000
Number of Foundations	39	19	5	21	84
FEE PER BOARD MEETING					
Low	200	100	50	100	50
High	3,100	1,000	3,000	500	3,100
Median	600	500	450	275	500
Number of Foundations	30	20	16	16	82
FEE PER COMMITTEE MEETING					
Low	200	100	15	100	15
High	900	800	1,000	100	1,000
Median	500	275	200	100	500
Number of Foundations	22	12	8	1	43

The dollar value of fees has roughly kept pace with inflation. Median fees on an annual basis have increased from $3,000 in 1980 to $5,000 in 1988; the per board meeting and per committee meeting increase has been from $250 to $500.

It should be noted that 38 percent of the foundations in the Council's 1988 survey reimburse board members for attending board meetings. Sixty-three percent reimburse board members when traveling to attend other meetings on behalf of the foundation or for professional development related to their foundation role.

The Case for Compensation

Several arguments are offered in support of the practice of paying honoraria (as defined on page 97) to foundation trustees.

(1) Many foundations are established in the form of trusts, and American law not only permits the payment of fees to the trustees of charitable trusts, but also defines the amount permissible. Most

state laws governing such payments were written before the era of large trusts, with the result that permissible fees are often outrageously high. The trustees of foundations set up in corporate style have the same responsibilities as trustees of foundations in the form of trusts. Why should they not receive similar treatment? Furthermore, if banks and trust officers are justified in charging foundations for their services as trustees, why should not individual trustees receive comparable compensation?

(2) The directors of corporations receive fees for their service on corporate boards—in many cases, quite handsome fees. Most foundations are legally organized as corporations, and the large ones tend to be managed in corporate fashion. A large number of foundation trustees are drawn from the world of corporate business and finance. Indeed, as we saw in chapter 5, this concentration is one of the criticisms leveled at foundations. To some of these individuals (by no means very many), it apparently seems appropriate to be as well compensated for serving on one board as on the other, even though they would not think staff salaries in the nonprofit world should match those of the business world.

(3) The Tax Reform Act of 1969 constituted the continental divide in the foundation world. Before that time, foundation trustees functioned in a relatively free and easy climate with few restrictions and few penalties. Since that date, the business of managing a foundation has become much more complicated and the penalties for mismanagement much more serious. Fee payment provides both compensation for work and inducement to serve.

(4) With diversification of board composition, compensation may become an important consideration in persuading individuals to accept membership. The traditional type of trustee drawn from the top echelon of society could afford to donate his or her time. The new trustees representing other segments of society may not be able to serve without compensation. It was this consideration that led the trustees of the Carnegie Corporation some years back to institute a $250 per meeting honorarium for all trustees.

(5) Service as a trustee is, or should be, time consuming. This obviously varies with the number and length of meetings, com-

mittee service, and premeeting preparation. An annual fee or
retainer has the advantage of creating or strengthening the moral
obligation to do one's duty. "The promise of such compensation,"
writes Zurcher, "would make it clear to board members that if
they accepted the responsibilities of membership they would have
to sacrifice a good deal of time and engage in serious effort. It
would fortify the chairman of the board or his alter ego, in demanding study and thought by board members over protracted
periods."[3]

(6) Although it is rarely expressed, there is the assumption on
the part of trustees that the foundation can well afford to pay
them for their services, since the foundation is a preexistent body
of money. Unlike most nonprofit organizations, foundations, at
least the private variety, do not have to raise each year all or
some part of their annual budgets. Community and other public
foundations do face the problem of raising funds, which explains
in part why few of them provide trustee compensation.

The Case Against Compensation

There are two compelling arguments against compensation for
trustees. If they are not completely convincing, nevertheless they
deserve the most careful attention by trustees.

(1) The first is the reduction in funds available to the beneficiaries of the foundation, the income from which is committed
to serving public needs. Some allowance for overhead and for
management and investment expense needs to be made as the
cost of doing business. But Section 4941 of the Internal Revenue
Code prohibits excessive compensation to staff by way of salaries
and perquisites, to consultants and advisers through fees, and to
trustees in the form of fees and honoraria. While "excessive" is
not defined, it could be argued that anything more than nominal
payments to trustees *for their service as trustees* would be excessive.

(2) Alexis de Tocqueville wrote 150 years ago in his justly
famous *Democracy in America* about the importance of voluntary
associations for the health of American society. Today, 800,000

---

[3] *The Management of American Foundations*, New York University Press, 1972,
p. 39.

nonprofit organizations and agencies constitute a third sector along with business and government. Many are staffed by volunteers, and with few exceptions all are governed by men and women who donate their time and service as a contribution to the common good. College and university trustees carry increasingly heavy responsibilities. So do the trustees and directors of museums, hospitals, symphonies, social welfare agencies, and many others. They serve *pro bono publico,* mostly without even reimbursement for expenses. Why should foundation trustees be an exception? What is happening to the great principle of volunteering?

How Much Is Enough?

Even though compensation for philanthropic activities has not been in the American tradition, as Young contends, it may well be that the tradition is eroding. We have no evidence that this is true of the nonprofit world in general, nor that the percentage of foundations providing honoraria is increasing greatly. If Andrews' 1969 findings can be trusted, approximately 500 foundations at that time compensated their trustees. The practice, however, is not likely to disappear altogether. Once it is accepted, the remaining question is, how much will the compensation be?

Trustees may perform a variety of professional services for their foundations, over and above those inherent in the role of trusteeship. Payments made to trustees for such services should be on the modest side and certainly no more than it would cost to obtain them from outside agents. (Some would argue that it is better to have all special services performed by outsiders in order to avoid any hint of self-serving.) Where payments to trustees run into six figures, as in the early years of the John D. and Catherine T. MacArthur Foundation and, more recently, the W. M. Keck Foundation, it is legitimate to wonder whether they are in the best interests of the foundations.

There remains, however, the basic question: What is a reasonable honorarium for a foundation trustee *as trustee*? The amount of time and thought devoted to this task will vary with the size of the grant program, with the policy of making a few large grants or many small ones, with the scope of the program, whether local, regional, national, or international; they will vary with the degree of commitment and concern of the trustees. Do they work at their job? Do they do their homework and attend meetings faithfully? The Ford Foundation trustees spend roughly four weeks a year in meetings (and this does not count the time spent on homework between meetings). Their annual honoraria averaging $12,000–13,000 are modest compensation for their service.

By the indenture establishing the Duke Endowment, James Buchanan Duke specified that three percent of the income of the endowment should be distributed equally among the fifteen trustees as compensation for their services. As a result, each of fourteen trustees (Doris Duke declined) received in 1987 payments in excess of $90,000. The Duke board meets ten times a year, and the members take their responsibilities seriously. The payments are entirely legal under the terms of the trust. In relation to the time involved, do they not seem excessive?

Even harder to justify are the fees paid to the trustees of the Keck Trust. For the calendar year 1980, Howard Keck and William M. Keck, the co-trustees of the trust for the benefit of the W. M. Keck Foundation, were paid $412,500 each. Although objections to the larger fees requested for this trust were made by the attorney general of California, the amount noted above was approved by Superior Court of California, County of Los Angeles, under the stipulation agreement agreed to by the trustees and the attorney general. The stipulation also contained a formula for calculation of future fee payments.[4]

---

[4] Subsequently, the attorney general in a letter to the Ways and Means Oversight Subcommittee dated August 2, 1983, stated in part: "This settlement formula . . . reflected a pragmatic compromise by this office to the prospect of repetitious litigation that already had consumed enormous time and resources of this office . . . We strongly disagree that the Attorney General's resolution of state court litigation in the W. M. Keck Trust should censor our expression of ongoing concern over one of the most extreme cases (sic) of high private foundation trustee's fees to come to our attention." This letter, the court order, the stipulation agreement, the testimony, and related documents are found on pages 100–116, *Tax Rules Governing Private Foundations*, Hearings before the Subcommittee on Oversight, June 27, 28, and 30, 1983, Part I, Serial 98–32.

There is no moral justification, whatever the law permits, for diverting more than a modest sum from beneficiaries of a foundation to the pockets of the trustees who are responsible for the charitable trust. Those who reject this position would do well to reflect on the ammunition that large payments to trustees can easily provide for the next populist attack on foundations.

CHAPTER 11

Full Disclosure: Public Right/ Foundation Need

We believe that full and early reporting of foundation activities not only serves the public right to know but can serve as one of the most powerful ways of attaining fuller accountability to the public. "Sunlight," as Justice Brandeis said, "can be the most powerful disinfectant." Government regulation can provide only a partial answer; the foundations themselves must realize that an informed and understanding public is essential.

PETERSON COMMISSION

For every foundation that has made strides in communications consciousness and action, others are still recalcitrant or simply mystified about the communications process. Some regard communications as an invasion of privacy; others as an unnecessary expense that diverts philanthropic dollars from charitable causes. Still others regard it as an occult, if not unsavory practice, more befitting show business and politicians than philanthropy.

RICHARD MAGAT

. . . in any clash between a private foundation's desire to maintain privacy and a reporter's desire for information about that foundation the foundation is invariably going to lose in the court of public opinion.

FRANK KAREL

Privacy and secrecy have, with notable exceptions, been characteristic of the foundation world. Under constant pressure, both from without and from within, they are opening up. One set of forces has been moral and legal; a second set, pragmatic.

Public Right to Know

If foundations are invested with a public interest, as argued in chapter 2, they are accountable to the public. They exist because the laws of the land permit them, and citizens determine the laws. Thus, trustees have an obligation to spread their activities and finances on the public record. Their half-private, half-public status exempts them from the sunshine laws, which require public bodies to open their meetings to the public, but it does not free them from their accountability to the public.

In spite of the fact that most foundations have been created under various state statutes, most state provisions for registration and supervision have been so inadequate that until fairly recently, many states did not have even an adequate roster of foundations. The federal government began requiring annual reports in 1942, but for many years returns on form 990-A were so incomplete, inadequate, or missing that IRS information and supervision were of little value. This situation changed with the passage of the 1969 Tax Reform Act (TRA).

That act required all foundations to file two forms (990-PF and 990-AR) with the IRS each year; to send copies to the state attorney general or secretary of state; to make available in the foundation's office for 180 days a copy of these forms for public inspection; and to place in a newspaper of general circulation a notice calling attention to the availability of the forms. An uncomfortable number of episodes suggest that some foundations have made it difficult, if not impossible, for individual inquirers to inspect the 990 forms in the foundation's office, but the magnificent work of the Foundation Center has done much to make the minimum information available, and the 1969 TRA has changed the picture with respect to reporting to the IRS.

Current regulations require the annual filing of a single form, the 990-PF, which calls for detailed and complicated reporting on "tax administration" information and "public" information.

Completion of this form each year is a complicated and difficult business. In 1983, the General Accounting Office made a study of the 990-PF returns for the years 1980 and 1981. It found a 98 percent completion rate of the tax administration section and a 70 percent failure to complete 25 percent or more of the items under public information. It turned out that many of the missing answers were the result of unclear instructions and the failure to follow up incomplete returns. The IRS has tightened its procedures, and the results are now presumably more satisfactory.

Practical Reasons for Public Disclosure

Apart from the moral and legal obligations to report, which apply to all foundations, there are several practical advantages to middle- and large-sized foundations in communicating with a variety of constituencies.[1]

(1) Trustees have frequently opposed publicity with the claim that they would be flooded with requests for grants, overloading their capacity to cope and increasing both their costs and the number of disappointed grant seekers. "The good news," writes Locke, "is that many foundations that do publish guidelines, annual reports, and other public statements are finding that, as a result of their communications, inappropriate requests are *decreasing*, and what is even better, the number of strong, creative proposals is *increasing.*"

(2) Reporting focuses attention on the direction and scope of foundation activities. Have the approved policies and guidelines been followed? Is the foundation headed in the right direction? The effort to explain the foundation to the public can become a kind of internal gyroscope or compass.

---

[1] The following arguments are drawn from the excellent articles of Elizabeth H. Locke, education and communications director for the Duke Endowment (*Grants Magazine*, December 1985); Frank Karel, former vice president for communications at the Robert Wood Johnson Foundation, now at the Rockefeller Foundation (*Increasing the Impact: 1980's*, published by the W. K. Kellogg Foundation); and Richard Magat, former president of the Hazen Foundation and currently Visiting Fellow at the Foundation Center (*Communications and Public Affairs Guide* in the Resources for Grantmakers Series, published by the Council on Foundations).

(3) Annual reports and other publications are a way of winning friends and influencing people. Sensitive trustees have been reluctant to seek credit for their good works and cite biblical authority for conducting their charity in secret. But this makes their foundations vulnerable to the attacks of the uninformed. What shocked the foundation community in the 1968 and 1969 congressional hearings was the almost total absence of understanding, on the part of both the public and the Congress, of what foundations were, what they stood for, what they did, how they operated, and the likely social costs of their demise. And for this, the trustees of foundations had themselves to blame. If we refuse to tell people what we do, we cannot expect to have friends in time of need. If we maintain a high wall of secrecy around ourselves, we invite people to suspect that we have something improper to hide. If we refuse to respond to inquiries, we shall make enemies rather than friends.

(4) The case for periodic evaluations of grant programs was presented in chapter 9. The discipline necessary to writing an honest annual report is a salutary stimulus to such an assessment. What was actually accomplished during the past year or biennium? How close did we come to our goals? How many grants were successes, how many failures? It is important for trustees and staff to face this kind of balance sheet as well as to present it to the public. How else does one improve?

(5) The above four advantages look inward; they suggest ways of improving foundation performance or survival. The following three look outward. Publicity for foundation grants can be an enormous asset to the grant recipients. Some are too small, too poor, too unsophisticated to generate much publicity for themselves. Public attention invites support from other quarters or cooperation from other agencies. To quote Locke again: "Promotion on behalf of a successful grantee is often a gift of equal value to the grant, yet it often costs the foundation next to nothing."

(6) Publicity focuses attention on important problems of society and thereby encourages support from other sources. In "Who Can Hear a Tree Falling?" Karel and Weisfeld describe the great lengths to which the Robert Wood Johnson Foundation goes to

communicate its work in the health field because the issues are so important and because they hope that others will find better solutions.[2]

(7) The results of foundation grantmaking can be exciting and heartwarming. They ought to be known for their own sake. But they ought to be known as testimony to the importance of philanthropy in our society "as a rich alternative and complement to other sectors of American society," in the words of Richard Magat.

The Performance Record

How well are foundations actually doing? The following table from the 11th edition of *The Foundation Directory* tells the story:

NUMBER OF FOUNDATIONS THAT ISSUE PUBLICATIONS

	Number of foundations	Number issuing publications	Percent	Number issuing annual reports	Percent
$100 million and over	142	122	85.9	98	69.0
$50–$100 million	127	95	74.8	67	52.8
$25–$50 million	200	114	57.0	74	37.0
$10–$25 million	586	286	48.8	143	24.4
$5–$10 million	694	238	34.3	98	14.1
$1–$5 million	2,661	544	20.4	199	7.5
Under $1 million	738	156	21.1	63	8.5
All directory foundations	5,148	1,555	30.2	742	14.4

While 30.2 percent of all *Directory*-size foundations issue some kind of publication, these represent 76 percent of total assets and 72 percent of total grants; likewise, the 14.4 percent issuing annual reports represent 62 percent of assets and 57 percent of grants of *Directory*-size foundations. (And *Directory*-size foundations represent 97 percent of all foundation assets and 92 percent of all foundation giving.) Recent years have seen a great improvement, but it remains disturbing that 14 percent of foundations with assets over $100 million and 25 percent of those in the next asset

---

[2] In *Increasing the Impact: 1980s*, published by the W. K. Kellogg Foundation, 1985.

size issue no publications to the public; 31 percent of the largest asset group and almost half of the next largest publish no annual reports.

Resistance to giving out information about themselves—even information that would seem to serve the foundation's ends—is reflected in the experience of the editors of the latest edition of the *Directory*, the standard reference work for the top 5,000 foundations. Only four percent responded fully to requests for information, forcing the editors to turn to IRS data of uncertain accuracy to complete the record. In a 1980 survey of the top 208 independent, community, and company-sponsored foundations, the National Committee for Responsive Philanthropy was unable to get information about their publications from 30 percent.[3]

Content of Annual Reports

Annual reports vary widely in size, format, and content. Some are elaborate and expensive; others consist of a single photocopied sheet or a pamphlet of four or six panels that can fit into a number 10 envelope. The format will be determined to a large extent by the scope and character of the foundation's program. If, for the moment, we disregard cost, what is the ideal content of an annual report? Margo Viscusi provides an excellent summary of essential information in the January/February 1985 issue of *Foundation News*. She suggests the following ten items:

1. Name, address, and telephone number of the foundation.

---

[3] As an agency highly critical of what it considers ultraconservative foundation practices, the NCRP is understandably not popular in some foundation quarters, and this may account for the refusal to cooperate on the part of nearly one-third of those addressed. This does not explain or justify, however, the attitude of two Oregon foundations that refused to provide information for the *Guide to Oregon Foundations* prepared in 1977 by the Tri-County Community Council. The chairman of one of the foundations threatened to withdraw support for the United Way on which the Community Council was heavily dependent if his foundation was mentioned in the *Guide*. As a result, the *Guide* omitted information publicly available through 990 forms. The protesting foundations were included in the 1981 edition of the *Guide*. For further information see NCRP: *Foundations & Public Information: Sunshine or Shadow?*, 1980; and *Oregon Foundations: Private Sector Response to Public Needs*, published by the Portland Committee for Responsive Philanthropy, pp. 7–8.

2. Name of each trustee with current affiliation and/or address.
3. Name and title of each staff member.
4. Statement of the foundation's purpose.
5. Statement about its current grants program—subject areas, kinds of support, limitations on funding.
6. Instructions on how to apply for a grant—person to contact, deadlines for submission, special application forms.
7. Statement on how, by whom, over what period of time requests are reviewed, funding decisions made, and grant applicants notified.
8. A list of grants made in the reporting period with amount of grant, purpose and length of grant, and grantee's address.
9. Complete financial statement for the reporting period plus an auditor's report.
10. List of the foundation's investments.[4]

This is a fairly tall order and well beyond the capacity of the vast number of small foundations. Most of the information, however, can be succinctly stated on one to three pages. The Council on Foundations has a simple set of guidelines for minimal reports, and the Communications Network in Philanthropy has developed, in conjunction with the Council, a Communications Assistance Service to assist foundations with their publications. In discussing the importance of their annual reports in 1979, C. S. Harding Mott, now chairman emeritus, and William S. White, chairman and president, wrote:

> We recognize that annual reporting may seem overwhelming to the small or newly emerging foundation, especially if they have little or no staff. Yet the document does not have to be complex: It should be commensurate with a foundation's size and activity. (We recognize that a majority of foundations are small, non-staffed, and give to a few charities. In some cases, they are conduits through which the donors can channel their money to charity.) A young foundation does not have to distribute thousands of copies of its report: the local library, grant recipients, and the Foundation Center could be primary audiences at first.

---

[4] P. 30–35. Margo Viscusi, past president of the Communications Network in Philanthropy, is currently director of publications for Hunter College.

The Mott Foundation has a standing offer to help any foundation with its first annual report, as do other members of the Communications Assistance Service, including the W. K. Kellogg Foundation, the Robert Wood Johnson Foundation, and the Chicago Community Trust.

In 1983 the Council established the Wilmer Shields Rich Awards for Excellence in Annual Reports to encourage and exhibit outstanding annual reports, to underline their importance, and to commend efforts at increasing communications in the grantmaking community. The judges evaluate the reports for the clarity and thoroughness of the information they present for grantseekers (and the potential donors in the case of community foundations) and for their success in attaining the goal of public accountability. Judges also consider the reports' readability (language, organization), use of enhancing graphics and design, and overall impact in communicating the grantmaker's interests to its constituencies.[5]

It is perhaps only fair to note that Waldemar A. Nielsen, author of two major studies of the largest foundations, holds a dissenting view on the importance of annual reports. He finds them "ill designed and inefficient vehicles to accomplish most of the purposes intended." He finds too many of them uninformative and misleading. Some reports consist of bland generalities, signifying nothing. Some present one-sided pictures by including only successful ventures. If foundations do not make mistakes, they are not taking enough risks and the failures need to be reported along with the successes. Nielsen is right in calling attention to the wide range of other publications and methods of communication that the more imaginative foundations are adopting. But his disparagement of annual reports because of their past inadequacies misses the point. The answer to poor reports is good reports.[6]

---

[5] See Tom Stamp: "Searching for Excellence," in *Foundation News,* July/August 1987, p. 36.

[6] See chapter 16, "Public Reporting: The Enclave Mentality," in *The Big Foundations,* Columbia University Press, 1972; and pp. 416–417 in *The Golden Donors,* E. P. Dutton, 1985.

Reports should be written and distributed with a clear idea of the audience they are aimed at. A small foundation with local and limited charitable interests has a much smaller constituency than the giant foundations with national and international concerns. As noted above, an annual report can consist of two or three photocopied pages or of a single sheet folded to form six panels. It need not cost much to produce, and distribution will be relatively small.

Other Forms of Communication

There are other ways of telling one's story than in the annual or periodic report. Some foundations use newsletters in place of or in addition to reports. Others use the special report format to call attention to an important problem or to one or more programs designed to deal with such a problem.

Another form of communication is the open or public meeting. The Donee Group recommended to the Filer Commission "that the law require annual public meetings of the governing boards of grantors with $250,000 or more in assets or $100,000 or more in total grants per year," and the Filer Commission endorsed this recommendation in its final report.[7] This was not met by any burst of enthusiasm from the foundation world. The Bush Foundation, however, the second largest in Minnesota with assets over $300 million, took up the challenge. It scheduled an open meeting for October 5, 1976, in a downtown St. Paul auditorium, mailed out 5,000 invitations to applicants, beneficiaries, other foundations, public officials, and the press, and it issued invitations to all and sundry through public announcements. Four hundred and fifty people showed up for a half-hour presentation followed by an hour of lively questions and answers.

The experiment was so successful that the following year the Minnesota Council on Foundations initiated a series of open meetings designed "to provide more specific information to the public on foundation activity and corporate giving." With varying

---

[7] Op. cit., p. 23 for the Donee statement. See *Giving in America,* p. 166, for the Filer Commission position.

formats, these meetings have continued on an annual basis. The idea is slowly catching on. Several regional associations of grant-makers now hold periodic "Meet the Grantmakers" sessions, to which the public is encouraged to come to hear foundation and corporate leaders discuss their operations.

Foundations have perhaps been slower than other nonprofit organizations to take advantage of electronic technology to present their story, but more and more are beginning to use film clips, tapes, and videocassettes. They are a graphic way of reporting on the results of some of their grants. In the November/December 1987 issue of *Foundation News*, Elizabeth H. Locke, director of the education division and communications at the Duke Endowment, tells the story of the Foundation Center's creation of a documentary film about foundations. Under the leadership of the Endowment, several foundations joined in financing the documentary, which runs 28 minutes and is available to foundations and the public.

Sources of Public Information

In theory, information about the governing boards, purposes, restrictions, assets, and grants of the 25,000 foundations in the United States is available to the general public.

For 30 years the Foundation Center in New York has been the major source of information, maintaining a complete, or as complete as possible, roster of foundations. It maintains two national libraries, one in New York and the other in Washington, two regional libraries in Cleveland and San Francisco, and over 170 cooperating libraries scattered across the United States with local directories and 990-PF returns for foundations in their states or regions. The Foundation Center's data are also available to grant-seekers and others through the computerized Dialog information system. In addition, the Foundation Center publishes *The Foundation Directory*, which is referred to frequently in this study, and an impressive variety of additional source books and treatments of special topics of interest to grantmakers and grantseekers.

The Council on Foundations, with membership around 1,100 grantmaking organizations and headquarters in Washington, is the major forum for the discussion of foundation concerns. Its *Foundation News* and *Newsletter* keep trustees and staff up-to-date. It publishes a biennial *Foundation Management Report;* periodic reports on compensation; a *Resources for Grantmakers Series* dealing with timely issues; and special studies on community foundations, company-sponsored foundations, public policy issues, etc. It holds an annual conference and many smaller and often regional conferences to assist trustees and staff.

Add to all this the many publications and meetings of the regional associations of grantmakers. Add also the growing number of commercial publications about foundations aimed at grantseekers, and the problem is less lack of information than too much. Sophisticated grantseekers have no trouble in finding out what they need to know. Unsophisticated seekers, however, outnumber them. The general public does not know how to make use of the many sources of information. Neither members of Congress nor the media are likely to spend much time in foundation research.

The story on foundations needs to be told in ways that reach many audiences. Foundations are improving. In their own self-interest, they need to do more.

CHAPTER 12

What Doth the Law Require?

In a democracy regulations are a form of social discipline which define the parameters of the public interest. So like other areas of private activity endorsed and enhanced by public policy, private foundations are now a regulated industry subjected to periodic public scrutiny.

JAMES A. JOSEPH

Many forms of conduct permissible in a workaday world for those acting at arm's length, are forbidden by those bound by fiduciary ties. A trustee is held to something stricter than the morals of the market place. Not honesty alone, but the punctilio of an honor the most sensitive, is then the standard of behavior. As to this there has developed a tradition that is unbending and inveterate.

JUDGE CARDOZO

Any study of the responsibilities of foundation trustees must go well beyond the legal requirements, but it would be a mistake to overlook the fact that many of those responsibilities are rooted in law, both common and statutory. There is a well-defined body of law related to trusts. The laws governing charitable corporations, however, are still evolving and vary from state to state. The directors of these charitable corporations, widely called trustees, share with the trustees of charitable trusts the position of fiduciary. "The fiduciary relationship," writes Marion R. Fremont-Smith, "arises in many different situations, and although it is considered to be most intense in the trust, directors and officers of corporations are also fiduciaries. Their legal duties have been developed from the same principles as those applicable to trustees."[1]

It is important for foundation trustees not only to be familiar with the various legal requirements and restrictions within which they must operate, but also to understand when and how they came about. And since "private foundations will continue to be the most closely monitored and scrutinized charitable organizations in the eyes of Congress,"[2] the historical background should help trustees cope with new efforts at government regulation.

Brief History of Government Regulation

In spite of hostile investigations by the Walsh Commission in 1916, the Cox Committee in 1952, and the Reece Committee in 1953, foundations enjoyed relatively little government regulation before 1969. A 1943 Revenue Act required foundations to file annual reports, and one in 1950 restricted self-dealing to arm's length transactions and denied tax exemption for unreasonable accumulations of income, but the IRS was not equipped to provide serious enforcement. In 1954 Congress revised the tax code and the Tax Code of 1954, as amended, has served as the basic document and reference ever since.

The 1969 Tax Reform Act

The era of benign neglect ended with the Tax Reform Act of 1969, which was largely the result of an unrelenting attack on foundations during the 1960s by Congressman Wright Patman. The number of questionable and illegal practices was not great, but the abuses were real—and indefensible. The restrictive, and at points punitive, 1969 TRA was the result. In retrospect, what seemed at the time to border on disaster has turned out to have more positive than negative results. In details it is a mixed bag. Overall it has done more than anything else to bring home to all

---

[1] *Foundations and Government*, Russell Sage Foundation, 1965, p. 134. This is an excellent and comprehensive treatment of the subject.

[2] John A. Edie in *America's Wealthy*, p. 64. I am much indebted to his chapter, "Congress and Foundations: Historical Summary" and to his *Congress and Private Foundations: An Historical Analysis*, Edie, John A., 1987, for the following section.

foundation trustees what most already knew and acted upon, i.e., that they must act more responsibly in the public interest.

The act defined private foundations for the first time and distinguished between them and public charities, which, along with operating foundations, were given more favorable treatment. Tax deductible gifts in cash to private nonoperating foundations were limited to 20 percent of income as against 50 percent for public charities and operating foundations; gifts of appreciated property were limited to 20 percent for private foundations, 30 percent for the others. The fair market value was allowed for gifts to public charities, but only cost plus 60 percent of gain for gifts to private foundations.[3]

The 1969 TRA imposed for the first time an excise tax of four percent on foundation income, ostensibly to cover the costs of monitoring foundations and administering the new regulations. This was reduced to two percent in 1978 and in 1984 to one percent for those foundations that could meet quite stringent conditions. Private foundations are the only nonprofit organizations required to pay an excise tax, and currently the tax at two percent generates six times the amount the IRS expends for supervision of the whole Exempt Organizations Division.

To force foundations to increase their total giving, the act set a variable minimum payout for every foundation beginning at six percent of assets or net income, including realized capital gains, whichever was larger. When evidence accumulated that this formula was slowly eroding foundation assets and would ultimately be disastrous, the law was changed in 1976 to require a payout of five percent of assets or net income, whichever is larger, and in 1981 to a flat five percent.

All acts, including arm's length, of self-dealing were proscribed by the act. Disqualified persons in such dealing included almost everyone who had any connection with the foundation, together with the family of such individuals. Penalties were set for violations.

---

[3] No restrictions were placed on gifts by bequest, which are tax free to both public and private charities.

To prevent control of a business through foundation stock ownership, the act prohibited the foundation and all disqualified persons from owning more than 20 percent of a business (up to 35 percent under certain circumstances). For some foundations whose portfolios were heavily concentrated in certain areas—e.g., Kellogg and MacArthur—this proved to be a real hardship, but most efforts to modify the proscription have been unsuccessful.

Penalties were set for investments jeopardizing the foundation's assets and consequently its income, and also for unreasonable fees and other administrative expenses.

The act reaffirmed the prohibition against grants for political purposes and for lobbying, established new requirements for grants to individuals, and required "expenditure responsibility" for grants to other foundations and to non-501(c)(3) organizations.

Finally, the 1969 TRA imposed detailed financial and grant-making accounting through a revised 990-PF form and a new 990-AR form. These were combined in a once again revised 990-PF in 1980.

Recent Tax Law Changes

For better or for worse, the 1969 TRA changed the foundation landscape. With only minor adjustments, the government and the foundations spent the following fifteen years getting used to the new arrangement. In 1983 the House Ways and Means Committee decided to take a fresh look at foundations and the non-profit world. The Subcommittee on Oversight of the House Ways and Means Committee, with Representative Charles B. Rangel as chair, held hearings. Alerted well in advance and well-organized, the Council on Foundations, Independent Sector, and other non-profit associations and agencies deluged the subcommittee with evidence. The climate was as friendly as the 1969 hearings had been hostile.

Foundations did not get all they wanted. The 1984 Deficit Reduction Act allowed an extension under certain circumstances for divestiture of excess holdings, but did not modify the basic law. It did provide for a reduction of the excise tax from two percent to one percent, but under conditions that make it difficult for many foundations to take advantage of the change.[4] It softened a bit the disadvantage of private foundations in receiving gifts, raising tax deductible gifts of cash to 30 percent of income, allowing a five-year carryover of any excess, and permitting gifts of publicly traded stock to be deducted at full market value. It redefined substantial contributors and family members in ways to ease the burden on foundations.

The act imposed one new restriction on foundations. Previous regulations had permitted administrative costs as well as grants to be included in the five percent payout. Apparently disturbed by evidence that administrative costs constituted a disproportionate share of the payout, Congress limited the amount of grant administrative costs that could qualify to 0.65 percent of asset value. Foundations are not denied the right to spend more on administration, but they are penalized to the extent that the excess over 0.65 percent of assets may not count toward the required five percent payout.[5]

State Regulation

Foundations, whether they are in the form of trusts or of charitable corporations, are subject to state as well as federal regulation, and the laws vary from state to state. In some jurisdictions, state probate courts or courts of equity have supervisory authority, but in general the state attorneys general have primary responsibility for oversight and control. In theory they represent the public, or the beneficiaries for whom the foundations were established, and have the right to intervene when questions of legality or propriety are raised. Some examples of this will be discussed later in the chapter.

Having little information on which to act during the first half of the century, attorneys general paid scant attention to foundations, but in recent years they have assumed increasingly im-

---

[4] See Norman A. Sugarman: "New Law Could Backfire," *Foundation News,* January/February 1985.

[5] For details, see John Edie: "New Tax Bill Creates Crucial Changes in Tax Return," in *Foundation News,* November/December 1984, pp. 48–49. What counts and does not count in calculating administrative costs demands careful study.

portant roles. A Uniform Supervision of Trustees for Charitable Purposes Act was drafted in 1954, approved by the American Bar Association, and subsequently adopted with variations by a number of state legislatures. It called for the registration of foundations and the filing of annual reports in the attorney general's office. This flow of information was further increased by the 1969 TRA requirement that copies of the federal 990 forms should be made available to appropriate state officers. State supervision has been steadily growing, but it is interesting to note that according to David Ormstedt of the Office of the Attorney General, State of Connecticut, while 32 states register soliciting charities, only twelve states require registration of private foundations.

Loyalty to Donor and to Foundation Charter

From a legal point of view, there are two basic responsibilities of trustees: loyalty to the donor's intent and loyalty to the beneficiaries, both of which involve adherence to the letter and the spirit of the law. Let us begin with the first.

The donor or donors always have some philanthropic purpose in mind in creating a foundation. That purpose may be as broad as the welfare of mankind or as narrow as the continued support of a single school or hospital or religious institution. In broad purpose, foundation trustees are relatively free to use their own best judgment; indeed, they are obligated to decide within the framework of their charter how foundation grants will maximize the public good. In some cases the donor or donors may indicate their special concerns by active participation in early board decisions, as did Carnegie and Rockefeller. In others the donors may have expressed, either orally or in writing, nonbinding preferences that trustees are likely to interpret as moral, although not legal, instructions. Still others, like William L. McKnight of the McKnight Foundation or MacArthur of the John D. and Catherine T. McArthur Foundation, may leave the disposition of their foundations' grantmaking entirely to the trustees.[6]

---

[6] "I figured out how to make the money. You fellows will have to figure out how to spend it" is the instruction MacArthur, more interested in tax avoidance than in philanthropy, is alleged to have given his legal counsel who drew up the plan for the foundation.

Most trustees would like to feel that they are carrying out the wishes of the donor. Intimate knowledge of the donor's convictions and ways of thinking, whether as a business associate, close friend, or family member, can be of real help. But this relationship can be easily, although usually unconsciously, abused. Nonfamily trustees will often defer to the insistence of wife, son, or daughter that she or he knows better than anyone else what the donor would want, which, as time goes on, can unconsciously become what the wife, son, or daughter want. Nor is it always easy for trustees to recognize that with changing times the donor's interests would also have changed, so that slavish adherence to past interests would fail to carry out the donor's larger intent.

Special purpose foundations sometimes present a different problem. It is not always possible for trustees to continue to carry out the specific purposes set forth in the charter, either because they are too narrowly defined or because unanticipated changes in society make "ancient ways uncouth." The White–Williams Foundation, referred to in chapter 3, is a case in point. In this situation trustees may have no alternative but to seek court approval for deviations from specific requirements through the doctrine of *cy pres* to alter the original purposes, keeping as close as possible to the spirit of the donor's intent.

Community foundations have greater flexibility than private foundations in this regard. Designed to serve the changing needs of local communities, community foundations accept designated funds only with the proviso that the trustees or distribution committee members may alter the purposes under certain circumstances. Indeed, this variance power is a central requirement of the community foundation, which, according to current Treasury regulations, must have the authority

To modify any restrictions or condition on the distributions of funds for any specified charitable purposes or to specified organizations if in the sole judgment of the governing body such restriction or condition becomes, in effect, unnecessary, incapable of fulfillment, or inconsistent with the charitable needs of the community or area served.

Buck Trust Issue

A classic case of loyalty to the donor's intent was fought out in the Buck Trust dispute in California during the years 1984–1986. Beryl Buck died in 1975, bequeathing to the San Francisco Foundation a gift of stock in the Belridge Oil Company valued at $10.9 million. Her will provided that the income should be used "for exclusively non-profit, charitable, religious or educational purposes in providing care for the needy in Marin County, California, and for other non-profit charitable, religious or educational purposes in that county. . . ." By the time the assets of the Buck Trust were turned over to the San Francisco Foundation in 1980, they were worth $260 million, and by 1986 they had grown to over $400 million, with annual income in excess of $30 million.

The unanticipated size of the trust, its limitation to Marin County, the second wealthiest county per capita in the United States, plus the pressing needs in the other four Bay Area counties served by the San Francisco Foundation, troubled the foundation's distribution committee and led to discussion with the state attorney general about the possibility of invoking the foundation's variance power. In January 1984, the committee filed a petition with the Marin Superior Court to modify the terms of the trust through the *cy pres* doctrine to permit grants outside Marin County. The *cy pres* principle is normally applied when the terms of a trust become "illegal, impossible or impracticable." The distribution committee stated in connection with its petition:

> The Distribution Committee is aware that our decision has momentous consequences for all philanthropy, as well as for the future standing of The San Francisco Foundation. It is only after more than three years of carefully monitoring the growth of the Buck Trust and the resulting grants program, consulting with experts and engaging in internal discussion and debate that we have reached the decision to ask the Court to allow us to spend some of the revenue from the Buck Trust outside Marin County.

There followed a bitter lawsuit in which the attorney general, Mrs. Buck's lawyer and executor, and Marin County opposed the petition and requested the court to remove the San Francisco Foundation as trustee of the Buck Trust. (Other interested parties joined in the suit both for and against.) The foundation argued (1) that Mrs. Buck had indicated a general charitable interest, (2) that she could not have anticipated the extraordinary increase in the value of her bequest, and, (3) therefore, that the explicit limitation of her philanthropy to Marin County was impracticable and an inefficient use of charitable funds. The attorney general and the executor countered (1) that the foundation had violated its responsibility to administer the trust in accordance with the terms of the will, (2) that it had failed to prove that the terms of the trust could not be carried out (not denied by the foundation), and, (3) therefore, that the petition should be denied and the foundation removed as trustee. During the course of the trial, various formulae for compromise were proposed by the judge and rejected by one party or the other.

Rulings by the judge adverse to the foundation's case finally led to a settlement. Its terms provided that the San Francisco Foundation resign as trustee for the Buck Trust; that a court-designated Marin Community Foundation be empowered to distribute the income from the trust for the benefit of Marin County; that 20 percent of annual income be set aside for one to three major projects "to be located only in Marin County, the benefits from which will inure not only to Marin County but to all mankind"; and that a special master be appointed by the court to monitor the settlement between the San Francisco and Marin County Foundations and to supervise and report to the court the operations of the latter.[7]

The charges and countercharges make sober reading, and the issues raised by the case should be weighed carefully by any board of trustees considering changes in the terms of their foundation's charter. The settlement was a victory for the primacy of the donor's terms of gift. Many have also viewed it as a sad loss for the

---

[7] The extent of judicial oversight is further enhanced by the proviso that the major projects "will be selected by the Court on the basis of an evidentiary hearing to be conducted within one year of the date of the Settlement Agreement." This summary account is drawn from documents prepared by the San Francisco Foundation, the Northern California Grantmakers, and the orders of Judge Thompson of the Superior Court of the State of California, County of Marin, filed July 31, 1986.

efficient and prudent expenditure of charitable money for the greatest possible public good.

Loyalty to Beneficiaries

The second basic responsibility of a foundation trustee is loyalty to the beneficiaries of the trust. "Administration of the trust solely in the interest of the public is the *sine qua non* against which the foundation trustee's loyalty, his most fundamental duty owed the public, must be tested."[8]

While legal differences do exist between the responsibilities of the director of a corporation and those of the trustees of a trust, these tend to merge in the actual management of foundations. The director or trustee of a foundation established as a corporation has the same duty to safeguard the interests of the beneficiaries, as does the trustee of a foundation established as a trust. And this duty is the basis for many of the positions defended in the preceding chapters.

One aspect of this responsibility deserves special attention. Loyalty to the beneficiary requires the avoidance of anything approaching an act of self-dealing in financial matters and the avoidance of conflicts of interest in grantmaking.[9] The 1969 TRA, as noted earlier in this chapter, prohibited all acts of self-dealing, even where it could be demonstrated that such a transaction would be advantageous to the foundation. To avoid the risk of penalty taxes through inadvertent violation of the self-dealing regulations, every foundation should maintain on record a complete list of all disqualified persons. A further safeguard to officers and trustees is to obtain written professional advice that the action contemplated is legitimate, in which case even a later finding that

---

[8] Robert H. Mulreany: "Foundation Trustees—Selection, Duties, and Responsibilities," in *USLA Law Review*, May 1966, p. 1065.

[9] Note Marion R. Fremont-Smith's statement: "A trustee's interest must always yield to that of the beneficiary. The fact that a trustee acted in good faith in a transaction where there was a question of self-dealing or self-interest is not an adequate defense to a charge of violation of the duty of loyalty; neither is ignorance nor innocence. It is immaterial whether the beneficiary is damaged." *Foundations and Government*, Russell Sage Foundation, 1965, p. 94.

the action was an improper investment or a taxable expenditure should relieve the officer or trustee from the penalty tax.[10]

Conflicts of Interest

Another aspect of conflict of interest arises when a grantmaking trustee has a connection with the grant recipient. It is the rare foundation trustee who does not serve on one or more *pro bono publico* boards or committees or whose wife or husband or children do not so serve. Disappointed petitioners and people hostile to the "power" they believe foundations wield are quick to suspect favoritism or undue influence when they see the trustee of the granting foundation also sitting on the board of the recipient agency. In drawing up their code of conduct, the trustees of the Northwest Area Foundation addressed themselves squarely to this issue: "Private foundations must strive so far as possible to be above suspicion. It is not enough that the Directors and the Staff *believe* that they are operating from the highest motives, and that any particular action is innocent, regardless of its appearance. So far as possible, actions and relationships must avoid an appearance of impropriety which raises questions in the minds of the public."

More and more foundations are adopting written guidelines constituting a code of conduct for trustees or staff or both. Full disclosure of all outside affiliations is the most common recommendation. The Ford, Rockefeller, Cleveland, and Northwest Area Foundations, for example, require annually updated rosters of such connections. The Chicago Community Trust and Northwest Area Foundation require relevant business affiliations as well as nonprofit ties. Some stipulate that trustees with potential conflicts of interest shall not vote on the issue; others insist that such trustees shall absent themselves from the board discussion as well as at the final vote. The Charles Stewart Mott Foundation goes even further, recommending that "Foundation personnel (trustees, officers, and staff) should generally not be associated in a

---

[10] See Norman Sugarman: "Penalties on Foundations and Foundation Managers: How to Avoid Them" in *Proceedings of the Eleventh Biennial Conference on Charitable Foundations*, New York University, 1973, pp. 235–257.

controlling capacity such as a Board member or officer if this puts the person or a combination of Foundation-related persons in a dominant role, or as an employee, with any prospective or present grantee or recipient of an appropriation of the Foundation."[11]

Duty to Provide Responsible Management

This is an omnibus responsibility covering many facets of a foundation's operations, most of which have been discussed in preceding chapters. They include the determination of goals, policies, and programs within the terms of the charter. They require attention to administration—staff relations, personnel policies, overhead expenditures, accurate financial and grant records, evaluation of programs, and periodic reviews. All trustees should know, and should make certain that grant recipients know, what grants are intended to accomplish. Attention to the composition of the board, to the need for continuity and the desirability of renewal, is part of responsible trusteeship.

The management of the finances of the foundation is part of every trustee's duty. Reasonable care and skill are the generally accepted criteria:

> The only general rule as to investments which can be laid down is that the trustee is under a duty to make such investments as a prudent man would make of his own property having primarily in view the preservation of the estate and the amount and regularity of the income to be derived. . . . It involves three elements, namely care and skill and caution. The trustee must exercise a reasonable degree of care in selecting investments. He must exercise a reasonable degree of skill in making the selection. He must, in addition, exercise the caution which a prudent man would exercise where

---

[11] Most codes of conduct cover staff as well as trustees. Here again, full disclosure of any outside connections is the rule. While some foundations permit or indeed encourage staff members to be active in community organizations (San Francisco and Northwest Area, for example), others prohibit such connections (Cleveland). Outside fees to staff are proscribed in general. The Ford Foundation prohibits acceptance of fees for speaking, consulting, radio, and television appearances, but allows directors' fees and authors' royalties. Gifts of more than nominal value may not be accepted. Even honorary degrees must first have the approval of the president.

the primary consideration is the preservation of the funds invested.[12]

Some states have established by statute a legal list of securities in which trustees of charitable trusts may invest, but in general the prudent man doctrine is the norm. This doctrine would suggest a reasonable degree of diversity in the portfolio and the avoidance of speculative investments. The latter are prohibited by Section 4944 of the Internal Revenue Code with its proscription of any investment that might jeopardize the charitable purposes for which the foundation was established.

In a "Report to the Council on Foundations" in May 1987, Lester Salamon and Kenneth Voytek of the Johns Hopkins Institute for Policy Studies analyze foundation investment policy and performance, concluding:

> It thus seems clear that there are a large number of foundations performing well below their potential, either by choice or lack of understanding. These foundations tend to manage their assets in a relatively lackadaisical fashion, with little oversight or willingness to take risks. While their prudence guards these foundations against significant losses, it also prevents them from achieving the levels of growth that are available, and that other foundations have successfully pursued.
>
> Finally, the data presented here provide evidence that professionalization of the foundation investment management process pays dividends in terms of higher return rates and therefore increased resources for charitable endeavors. With notable consistency, the foundations with the more coherent strategies, the longer-term perspective, the greater willingness to accept some short-term risk, and the heavier reliance on professional advice generated higher rates of return.[13]

An instructive example of the problems and pitfalls is to be found in the case of *Lynch v. John M. Redfield Foundation*.[14] The

---

[12] Austin W. Scott: *The Law of Trusts*, Little, Brown & Co. 1956, cited by Mulreany, op. cit., p. 1068.

[13] *Managing Foundation Assets: An Analysis of Foundation Investment and Spending Policies and Performance*, The Foundation Center, 1989.

[14] 9 Cal. App. 3d 293. 88 Cal. Rptr. 86 (1970). Schweitzer, P. J.

foundation was created in 1940 for charitable purposes. The three trustees deposited income in a bank, which in turn made distribution to various beneficiaries upon authorization by the trustees. In the late 1950s, disagreement as to management and grants developed among the trustees. One trustee refused to attend meetings, declined to recognize the other two as trustees, tried to establish a new board without them, filed unsuccessful lawsuits to oust them as trustees, and notified the bank not to honor instructions from the other two. As a result, the bank in 1961 declined to issue further payments to beneficiaries without court orders or unless all three trustees concurred. Since the trustees could not agree, income piled up in a noninterest-bearing account in the bank.

The attorney general brought action in a local court on grounds that the trustees had failed to manage the funds of the foundation in proper fashion by allowing income to lie idle in a noninterest-bearing bank account and had failed to carry out the charitable purposes for which the foundation existed. The trial court removed the dissident trustee, but declined to surcharge the trustees for the amount of the lost income. Upon appeal to the higher court, "the court held that the directors of a charitable corporation were held to the same standard as that of a trustee, the prudent man investment rule, and that as a matter of law the directors breached this rule by failing to invest the income during the five-year period. The court further held that good faith on the part of the two directors was no defense where the action was based on negligence, and that even though the fault may have rested with one trustee only, all the trustees were liable for the damages caused by the negligent acts of their co-trustee." The appeal court then returned the case to the lower court to determine the exact date of the breach of trust and to surcharge the trustees accordingly.

Delegation of Authority

Should trustees make use of investment advice and counsel? "It is both more prudent and more profitable for trustees to manage and direct the experts rather than attempt to ride the interest-rate roller coaster themselves," writes John W. Byrd, Dallas pension and trust fund consultant.[15] This raises an interesting question. According to the law of trusts, a trustee may not delegate to others actions that he or she can reasonably be expected to perform. "In essence, this rule states a personal duty on the trustee to administer the trust. His must be the final responsibility and ultimate source of all decisions. He may delegate the performance of administrative tasks to others, may employ counsel, attorneys, accountants, or stock brokers to handle certain matters, and may entrust them with the property of the trust, but he must maintain at all times full responsibility for their acts."[16]

The law is slowly changing to take account of the need in a complex society for dependence on expert advice, but the fact remains that trustees will in the last analysis be held accountable and cannot plead the delegation of authority in self-defense.

Although the now-famous case of *Stern v. Lucy Webb Hayes National Training School for Deaconesses and Missionaries*, better known as the Sibley Hospital case, concerns the trustees of a nonprofit hospital, the principle involved is just as applicable to foundation trustees. The facts in the case are so pertinent to a variety of other situations and Judge Gesell's decision so important that all trustees would do well to familiarize themselves with it. The plaintiffs brought charges of conspiracy, mismanagement, nonmanagement, and self-dealing against certain of the trustees of the hospital. Judge Gesell did not find the defendants guilty of the first two charges, but did find them guilty of the last two. The five trustees who were the chief targets of the suit were all affiliated with one or more financial institutions with which the hospital had maintained significant ties, including low- or non-interest-bearing accounts of considerable size. Judge Gesell found them involved in self-dealing and conflict of interest, but declined to assess damages on the grounds that there was no evidence the hospital had suffered from their acts. In his order, he laid down strict rules for full disclosure and for complete accounting of all transactions between the hospital and any of the banks involved.

---

[15] "Who Minds Your Money?" in *Foundation News*, September/October 1987, p. 57.

[16] Fremont-Smith: op. cit., p. 95.

More important to our present concern was the charge of non-management. The five trustees were all members of the hospital board's investment committee, one was a member of the finance committee, and three were members of the executive committee. The hospital's operations were dominated by two trustees, the treasurer and the hospital administrator. For nearly ten years, neither investment nor finance committee met, with all investments instead being handled by the strong-willed treasurer and bank deposits by the two dominant trustees. Judge Gesell stated in his memorandum opinion:

> Trustees are particularly vulnerable to such a charge (failure to supervise the investments and even to attend meetings) because they not only have an affirmative duty to 'maximize the trust income by prudent investment,' but they may not delegate that duty, even to a committee of their fellow trustees. A corporate director, on the other hand, may delegate his investment responsibility to fellow directors, corporate officers, or even outsiders, but he must continue to exercise general supervision over the activities of his delegates. . . . Applying these standards to the facts in the record, the court finds that each of the defendant trustees has breached his fiduciary duty to supervise the management of Sibley's investments.

Finding that the hospital had suffered no material damage from the failure of its trustees, the judge made no surcharges, but specified a number of steps to be taken to prevent a recurrence of the fiduciary breach.

Responsibility for Public Accounting

We discussed this responsibility in the preceding chapter, and, therefore, little more needs to be said here. It is well to keep in mind that trustees have both a legal and a moral responsibility: the annual filing of the federal 990-PF form, plus whatever the state requires, and, except for the smallest foundations, the publication in one form or another of periodic reports to the public.

The 1976 Tax Act authorized the Treasury to set up an Exempt Organizations Division to monitor tax-exempt organizations, including foundations. Trustees of large foundations can expect IRS audits every two to four years; for smaller foundations, the expectation is every six to ten years. Trustees and staff must therefore be prepared for periodic government audits. The Council of Michigan Foundations has prepared an excellent set of guidelines for coping with audits, entitled "When the IRS Comes Calling—For Foundations, an Audit Is as Inevitable as Perpetuity and Excise Taxes. Knowledge of the Entire Process Can Keep You One Step Ahead of the IRS."[17]

Duty to Avoid Jeopardizing Tax-exempt Status

This is implicit in all the duties so far discussed, but it may be helpful to bring some of the dangers out into the open. Proper application must be made for both federal and state tax exemption. Formal notice of such status should be kept on file. Any changes from the original charter must be cleared with appropriate authorities. Annual reports must be filed with various officers, and a variety of other forms and reports duly made.

In addition, Section 4945 of the Internal Revenue Code identifies a number of areas as improper foundation concerns. One such restriction is on grants to individuals, such as scholarships, fellowships, prizes, and awards for scholarly studies. They are permitted only when based on ground rules approved in advance by the IRS. The restrictions under which such grants may be made are not onerous, however, and it is to be hoped that a traditional and valuable form of foundation philanthropy will not be seriously inhibited. But trustees should be careful to meet the technical requirements.[18]

Second, grants to other private foundations and to non-501(c)(3) organizations are "taxable expenditures," unless the

---

[17] Copies are available from the Council of Michigan Foundations, P.O. Box 599, Grand Haven, MI 49417. It also appeared in *Foundation News*, September/October 1986.

[18] Section 4945 of the Internal Revenue Code specifies different rules for public and private foundations. Two publications of the Council on Foundations are very helpful in explaining the conditions and procedures for grant programs for individuals. See: "A Guide to the Making of Grants to Individuals by Private Foundations," in the *Resources for Grantmakers* series, August 1987; and an October 1984 Memorandum entitled "Grants by a Community Foundation to Individuals."

granting foundation exercises a high degree of monitoring and followup on the use of the grant by the grantee organization. This is known as "expenditure responsibility." It has proved sufficiently complicated to drive many foundations away from grants of this sort, although others are finding that they can manage the supervision and live with the red tape without too great discomfort. Some foundations have sought to avoid expenditure responsibility by using a community foundation or other public charity (exempt from the provisions of Section 4945) as a conduit for grants to a non-501(c)(3) organization. There are right and wrong ways of doing this.[19]

A third restriction prohibits grants in support of candidates for political office. But what about grants to organizations that deal with some aspect or issue of public policy associated with a political figure? Some such organizations are fronts for political support and activity, and are therefore taboo;[20] others are genuinely independent public policy groups and as such are entitled to foundation support. In July 1987, James A. Joseph, president of the Council on Foundations, issued a memorandum on the subject, which included a list of questions a foundation should ask before reaching a decision. Copies are available from the Council.

A fourth area is lobbying. The 1969 TRA prohibited lobbying by private foundations, save in their own self-defense. Public charities, which include community foundations, were not so restricted, and prior to 1976 were not penalized so long as lobbying constituted no substantial part of their activities. Because of the vagueness of the phrase "no substantial part," the 1976 Tax Reform Act proposed an expenditure test as an alternative.[21]

---

[19] See John Edie: "Fiscal Agents Can Be Illegal," in *Foundation News,* May/June 1986.

[20] The most recent legal provisions are to be found in the Omnibus Reconciliation Act of 1987. See the Council's Washington Update, February 2, 1988, citing "Public Policy and Foundations: The Role of Politicians in Public Charities," Center for Responsive Politics, 1987.

[21] Twenty percent of the first $500,000 of exempt purpose expenditures, fifteen percent of the second $500,000, ten percent of the third, and five percent of the remainder, with an upper limit of $1 million.

However, the threat to private foundations remained, i.e., that the use of a foundation grant by a donee for lobbying purposes could be used to penalize the donor foundation. In 1977 the Council on Foundations obtained from the IRS a private letter ruling, known as the McIntosh ruling, to the effect that a private foundation would not be violating the IRS code if its grant was for general purposes and not earmarked for lobbying. In 1986— a decade after the 1976 legislation—the IRS finally issued a set of proposed regulations regarding lobbying so restrictive as to jeopardize many foundations for past grants. Prior to 1987 a grant for nonpartisan research on some issue of present or future legislative concern had been considered within the law. The proposed regulations specified that use of such research by any third party in connection with its lobbying activities would render the foundation's original grant illegal and subject it to penalties. A chorus of protests from the nonprofit world persuaded the IRS commissioner to schedule hearings in the spring of 1987. As a result of the hearings, the commissioner set up an Exempt Organization Advisory Group and promised to review the regulations. No decision had been reached by the time this book went to press.[22]

Responsibility for Fund Raising—Community Foundations

The trustees or directors of most nonprofit organizations are selected, in large part at least, for their capacity to give or help get financial support. One of the charms of foundation trusteeship is to be in the role of giving rather than soliciting money. To this, however, the trustees of community foundations are an exception.

Community foundations begin small. In a recent survey, one-third had assets under $1 million and 71 percent had assets under $5 million. A general rule of thumb holds that a community

---

[22] For the full story of this legal morass, see the several articles by John Edie and Will Broaddus in *Foundation News*, from the November/December 1986 issue to that of November/December 1987.

foundation needs at least $5 million in assets to reach the take-off point where its existence is assured and $10 million to be completely self-sustaining. Even so, in order to serve the community better, it will, or should, be constantly seeking additional funds. As a public charity, it must meet the public support test, which requires each year the raising of additional funds.

The solicitation of new assets is, therefore, an integral part of the responsibility of a community foundation trustee or distribution committee member. Executive directors can plan and manage fund-raising campaigns, but trustees are normally the most effective solicitors. Furthermore, trustees must decide what kinds of funds to solicit and accept—unrestricted endowments, designated funds, advised funds, permanent, or pass-through. They must decide what avenues to pursue and methods to employ—targeted prospects, community-wide advertising, encouragement of the transfer of private foundation assets, and/or the avoidance of competition for funds with the public charities they exist to help.

In recent years the number of community foundations has been rapidly growing, and so have their assets. Some of the major private foundations have been offering challenge grants to get new community foundations started or to help fledglings grow stronger. Community foundation governing boards must be doing something right.

D&O Liability Insurance

Some foundations take out directors and officers (D&O) liability insurance to protect them, and the foundation as well, against damages arising from unintentionally wrongful acts. Wrongful acts include "any breach of duty, neglect, error, misstatement, misleading statement, omission, or other acts done or wrongfully attempted."[23]

---

[23] This section relies almost exclusively on the comprehensive treatment set forth by John A. Edie, vice president and general counsel of the Council on Foundations, in his *Directors and Officers Liability Insurance,* published by the Council on Foundations in its Resources for Grantmakers Series, December 1984.

Lawsuits may be brought against a foundation and/or its trustees and officers for violations of federal and state laws covering negligence, breach of contract, failure to file information, conflict of interest, improper investments, improper expenditures, and other infringements. Suits may be initiated by the IRS, the state attorney general, a disaffected trustee or employee, or grant recipients or disappointed grantseekers.

On paper, this is a formidable array. In practice, foundation officers and trustees have had to contend with relatively few suits for damages, although penalties for willful or unintentional violations of IRS regulations have been increasing. In the 1970s the trustees of the Wilder Foundation and the Minnesota Foundation were unsuccessfully sued for several million dollars by a cancer scientist whose employment by the foundations was terminated. In 1974 a disappointed grantseeker sued—again unsuccessfully—a cluster of Buffalo-based foundations, which had declined to make scholarship grants to his son. In 1984 J. Roderick MacArthur, son of the founders of the big MacArthur Foundation in Chicago and trustee of the foundation, brought suit against eight of his fellow trustees for mismanagement of the foundation's assets. The suit was withdrawn shortly before his early death. These, plus the Redfield and Buck Trust suits discussed earlier in this chapter, are examples of what can occur. In an increasingly litigious society, the number may well increase. Consider the proliferation of lawsuits in the past two decades against college and university trustees.

Forty-three percent of the independent and community foundations responding to the Council's 1988 survey reported that they had D&O liability insurance—75 percent of those with assets over $100 million down to 27 percent of those with assets under $10 million. The total liability limit ranges from $15,000 to $75 million with a mean of $8.6 million and a median of $1 million. Cost ranged from $100 to $150,000 per year, with a median of $5,500. The larger and more complex foundations have the greatest need for the protection of liability insurance; the small foundations with few staff and noncontroversial grants have the least need. The trustees of each foundation will have to decide at what point liability insurance becomes cost effective.

In a special 1986 memorandum entitled "Legal Climate: Duty of Care," John Edie suggests that courts tend to follow the "business judgment rule" in dealing with the liability of nonprofit organizations and their directors and officers. According to this rule, foundation managers will presumably be judged to have acted properly if (1) they acted on an informed basis, (2) they acted in good faith, (3) they acted for what they considered to be the foundation's best interests, and (4) they acted without fraud or self-dealing. Courts will examine carefully the evidence in support of these assumptions. Did the trustees have sufficient information? Did they critically examine the information? Did they take sufficient time to reach a considered decision?

Edie proposes seven steps or practices that strengthen the claim of a trustee to have acted in an informed and responsible way. They should be kept in mind.

1. Attend most board meetings and meetings of committees on which one serves.
2. Read financial statements, budget proposals, and other reports.
3. Question such reports when obvious inconsistencies or other problems appear.
4. Take steps to investigate and rectify problems that appear.
5. Insist on advance notice to directors of any major item of business to be acted upon at the next meeting.
6. Request meaningful written material to directors in advance of the board meeting at which action is to be taken.
7. Insist that accurate, thorough records are kept of the decisions made and the process for reaching the decision.

CHAPTER 13

Summing Up

When you die and come to approach the judgment of Almighty God, what do you think he will demand of you? Do you for an instant presume that he will inquire into your petty failures or your trivial virtues? No! He will ask just one question: "What did you do as a trustee of The Rockefeller Foundation?"

FREDERICK T. GATES

As I see it, there is no other way that as few people can raise the quality of the whole American society as far and as fast as can trustees and directors of our voluntary institutions, using the strength they now have in the positions they now hold.

ROBERT K. GREENLEAF

Three convictions—premises if you will—underlie this study of foundation trustees. First, foundations are very important to American society. Second, foundation performance is falling short of its full potential. Third, trustees are the key to better performance.

Proposition One: Foundations Are Very Important to American Society

Philanthropy is very important to American society. Foundations are an important part of philanthropy. Therefore, foundations are very important to American society.

Only those on the far left who believe that the state should do everything will challenge the major premise, and the history of political institutions does not support their view. Others, however, will question the minor premise, pointing out (as noted in chapter

141

1) that foundation giving in 1987 was only seven percent of total philanthropy and that total philanthropy that year was only two percent of the Gross National Product. Government expenditures for health, education, and welfare, it could be argued, vastly exceed private philanthropy—so why be concerned over the minuscule contribution, relatively speaking, made by foundations?

One answer is that the reductions in federal and state aid of the 1980s make private philanthropy all the more important and that $6 billion in foundation grants is no insignificant sum. Indeed, the widely diversified world of nonprofit organizations would find it difficult to survive without foundation support. And the contribution of foundations to human welfare is an extraordinary record. This story has been told often enough to need no retelling here. American society would be far more flawed than it is without the past century of foundation study and support.

Foundations provide a multiple approach to society's problems. The diversity of 25,000 different and independent centers of decision is a national asset. Foundations are, after all, large and small, national and local, broad goal and special purpose, independent, company-sponsored, and community oriented. In their pluralism, they reflect virtually the entire spectrum of social, economic, and political philosophies.

Another foundation asset is their flexibility. They are, or can be, quick to meet new opportunities and challenges. If programs prove unsuccessful, they can readily change. Furthermore, they combine the compassion important in human relations with the thoughtful analyses essential to uncover the causes of social ills. The special genius of foundations is their intelligent and planned programs to enhance the public welfare.

Foundations address private action to the solution or amelioration of public problems. ". . . philanthropy is far more than grantmaking," writes Paul Ylvisaker. "It is a constitutional statement by society that there should be a private counterpart to the legislative process, a freestanding alternative that allows for independent considerations of the public needs."[1]

---

[1] *The Nonprofit Sector: A Research Handbook,* p. 376.

Proposition Two: Foundation Performance Is Falling Short of Its Full Potential

The foundation record is impressive, but have foundations done as well as possible? They have been criticized from the left as bastions of conservatism and from the right as centers of un-American ideas. If it is important that foundations reflect a wide range of viewpoints, it is inevitable that their grants will not please everyone. Even if this is conceded, are there ways, nevertheless, in which foundations have fallen short of realizing their full potential?

One such way stems from the nature of a foundation as a body of money created by our traditional economic system. Donors and governing boards have a natural inclination to defend that system and to support the establishment. It is healthy that some foundations do this, but it is also healthy that other foundations should question whether charity is an adequate substitute for social justice. We need both points of view; but as one reviews the foundation field, one is impressed by the conservative and conventional emphasis in grantmaking. Such grants are not bad; they do much good, or so we believe. But with a little more imagination and boldness, they could be better.

A second way in which foundations have fallen short is their failure to plan. Too many grants are made as the result of personal whim. Compassion, as we have noted, is an important attribute of foundation trustees, but one of the great advantages of foundations is their capacity to take the long view. To concentrate on one or more areas of concern and to mount a program aimed at changing them are to use the assets of foundations to their best advantage. Even the smallest family foundations can improve their performance by planning ahead.

A third shortcoming of foundations is their failure to cooperate—with each other, with the nonprofit world, and with government. There are many notable exceptions to this generalization, and in recent years the situation has definitely improved. Traditionally, however, foundations have been inclined to go it alone. Happily, they are now beginning to see the advantages of working together on common problems—sometimes in grantmaking, sometimes in collaborating with the recipients of their grants, sometimes in developing public policy, and sometimes in helping governmental agencies do a better job.

Finally, there has been a reluctance on the part of many trustees to recognize their *public* responsibility. This failure manifests itself in two ways. One is the failure to focus on present and future public needs. As businessman and philanthropist J. Irwin Miller said in an eloquent address to the 1984 Council on Foundations Annual Conference, "The world and its needs may be changing under our noses, but, if we neither look nor listen, we may spend our time and the money entrusted to us happily correcting yesterday's ills. . . . Our horizons are too close, our visions too dim. Unable to sense what may most need doing, we follow fashion."[2] The other is the failure of many foundations to disclose to the public the nature of their operations and to make themselves accessible to grantseekers. Here again, the situation is improving, but foundation performance still fails to live up to the highest standards.

Proposition Three: Trustees Are the Key to Better Foundation Performance

Boards control foundations, and the trustees set the operational style. Are grant decisions made in perfunctory or thoughtful fashion? Does everyone think alike, or are there constructive differences of opinion? Do trustees really work at their job? We all know that some boards of directors/trustees are better than others. What makes them so? The style of operation deserves serious thought.

To be as effective as possible, boards of trustees, we have argued, need a certain breadth. This will vary with the size of the foundation. A nonfamily member, even on the smallest foundation board, will provide not only a different perspective, but also a kind of legitimacy in terms of the public's stake in foundation decisions. Boards also need to plan for their renewal. The world changes, and fresh points of view are essential. Special board

---

[2] *Foundation News,* May/June 1984, pp. 19–20. This address is well worth reading by every trustee.

sessions devoted to long-range issues will help, but rotation of membership is more effective.

Above all, boards of trustees need, in Matthew Arnold's famous phrase, "to see life steadily and to see it whole." If society were perfect, there would be no needs requiring foundation grants. Much philanthropy seeks to alleviate suffering; while this is true of many foundation grants, the greatest contribution that foundations can make is to remove the causes of society's ills. This requires trustees to look at their world with a critical eye and to decide where their grants can provide the greatest leverage. The central task of foundation trustees is to help build a better world.

And finally, boards need to recognize their responsibility for the future of foundations. Robert L. Payton, director of the Indiana University Center on Philanthropy and former president of the Exxon Education Foundation, has called attention to the role American business played in the past hundred years in creating a system and climate favorable to the survival of corporations in contrast to the course followed by European business.[3] That is a lesson that foundation trustees need to study. The performance of each board enhances or diminishes the image and value of foundations as a whole. No man is an island unto himself. Or, as Alan Pifer puts it:

> We have in our charge a unique social invention for the common good, an institution eminently worth having and worth preserving. We must manage it for the maximum good of mankind in our time and we must make every effort to pass it along to the next generation strengthened from within and reestablished in the confidence of an informed and sympathetic public. That is our responsibility.[4]

Foundation trusteeship is a tall order. It is demanding, exciting, and rewarding. It has a dual character. On the one hand, it is responsible for the distribution of private money for purposes designated by the donor; on the other hand, it is an exercise in public responsibility for the good of society.

---

[3] See the Council on Foundations' publication, "Moral Obligation or Marketing Tool? Examining the Roles of Corporate Philanthropy," 1985, pp. 4–5.

[4] *Foundations on Trial,* Council on Foundations, 1970, p. 23.

APPENDIX

Council on Foundations
Recommended Principles and Practices for
Effective Grantmaking[1]

1. Whatever the nature of the entity engaged in private grant-making, and whatever its interests, it should seek to establish a set of basic policies that define the program interests and the fundamental objectives to be served.

2. An identifiable board, committee, or other decision-making body should have clear responsibility for determining those policies and procedures, causing them to be implemented, and reviewing and revising them from time to time.

3. The processes for receiving, examining, and deciding on grant applications should be established on a clear and logical basis and should be followed in a manner consistent with the organization's policies and purposes.

4. Responsive grantmakers recognize that accountability extends beyond the narrow requirements of the law. Grantmakers should establish and carry out policies that recognize these multiple obligations for accountability: to the charter provisions by which their founders defined certain basic expectations, to those charitable institutions they serve, to the general public, to the Internal Revenue Service, and to certain state governmental agencies.

5. Open communications with the public and with grantseekers about the policies and procedures that are followed in grantmaking is in the interest of all concerned and is important if the grantmaking process is to function well, and if trust in the responsibility and accountability of grantmakers is to be maintained. A brief written statement about policies, program interests, grantmaking practices, geo-

---

[1] Adopted 1984

graphic and policy restrictions, and preferred ways of receiving applications is recommended. Prompt acknowledgment of the receipt of any serious applications is important. Grantseekers whose programs and proposals fall outside the interests of the grantmakers should be told this immediately, and those whose proposals are still under consideration should be informed, insofar as is possible, of the steps and timing that will be taken in reaching the final decision.

6. Beyond the filing of forms required by government, grantmakers should consider possible ways of informing the public concerning their stewardship through publication and distribution of periodic reports, preferably annual reports, possibly supplemented by newsletters, reports to the Foundation Center, and the use of other communications channels.

7. The preservation and enhancement of an essential community of interest between the grantor and the grantee requires that their relationship be based on mutual respect, candor, and understanding with each investing the necessary time and attention to define clearly the purposes of the grant, the expectations as to reports related to financial and other matters, and the provisions for evaluating and publicizing projects.

    Many grantmakers, going beyond the providing of money, help grantees through such other means as assisting in the sharpening of the objectives, monitoring the performance, evaluating the outcome, and encouraging early planning for future stages.

8. It is important that grantmakers be alert and responsive to changing conditions in society and to changing needs and merits of particular grantseeking organizations. Responses to needs and social conditions may well be determined by independent inquiries, not merely by reactions to requests submitted by grantseekers. In response to new challenges, grantmakers are helpful if they use the special knowledge,

experience, and insight of individuals beyond those persons, families, or corporations from which the funds originally came. Some grantmakers find it useful to secure ideas and comments from a variety of consultants and advisory panels, as well as diversified staff and board members. In view of the historic underrepresentation of minorities and women in supervisory and policy positions, particular attention should be given to finding ways to draw them into the decision-making processes.

9. From time to time, all grantmaking organizations should review their program interests, basic policies, and board and staff composition, and assess the overall results of their grantmaking.

10. Beyond the legal requirements that forbid staff, board members and their families from profiting financially from any philanthropic grant, it is important that grantmakers weigh carefully all circumstances in which there exists the possibility of accusations of self-interest. In particular, staff and board members should disclose to the governing body the nature of their personal or family affiliation or involvement with any organizations for which a grant is considered, even though such affiliation may not give rise to any pecuniary conflict of interest.

11. Grantmakers should maintain interaction with others in the field of philanthropy including such bodies as regional associations of grantmakers, the Foundation Center, the Council on Foundations, and various local, regional, and national independent-sector organizations. They should bear in mind that they share with others responsibility for strengthening the effectiveness of the many private initiatives to serve the needs and interests of the public and for enhancing general understanding and support of such private initiatives within the community and the nation.

SOURCES OF QUOTATIONS AT BEGINNING OF EACH CHAPTER

CHAPTER 1

Dwight McDonald, *The Ford Foundation: The Men and the Millions,* Reynal & Company, 1956, p. 3.

Foundations, Private Giving, and Public Policy, The Report of the Peterson Commission, University of Chicago Press, 1970, p. 47.

CHAPTER 2

Stated at a meeting of foundation trustees in the Southwest.

Paul Ylvisaker, "Foundations and Nonprofit Organizations," chapter 20 in *The Nonprofit Sector: A Research Handbook,* Yale University Press, 1987, p. 376.

CHAPTER 3

John W. Gardner, in his review of 50 years of the Carnegie Corporation, *Annual Report,* 1961.

Frederick deW. Bolman, "The Need to Evaluate a Foundation" in *Foundation News,* January/February 1970, p. 20.

CHAPTER 4

Merrimon Cuninggim, *Private Money and Public Service,* McGraw-Hill Book Company, 1972, p. 253.

John H. Filer, at a meeting of Mid-Continent Foundations, printed in *Foundation News,* July/August 1981, p. 1.

CHAPTER 5

Lewis A. Coser, *Men of Ideas, A Sociologist's View,* The Free Press, 1965, pp. 338–339.

Alan Pifer, *Philanthropy in an Age of Transition,* The Foundation Center, 1984, p. 111.

CHAPTER 6

Ernest V. Hollis, *Philanthropic Foundations and Higher Education,* 1938, p. 94.

Wilbert E. Moore, in *Trusteeship and the Management of Foundations,* by Donald R. Young and Wilbert E. Moore, Russell Sage Foundation, 1969, p. 20.

CHAPTER 7

F. Emerson Andrews, *Philanthropic Foundations*, Russell Sage Foundation, 1956, p. 89.

Merrimon Cuninggim, *Letters to a Foundation Trustee*, The Center for Effective Philanthropy, 1986, p. 5.

CHAPTER 8

Dean Rusk, "Building a Professional Staff," in *Proceedings of the Second Biennial Conference on Charitable Foundations*, New York University, 1955, pp. 170–171.

Robert W. Bonine, "One Part Science, One Part Art," in *Foundation News*, November/December 1971, p. 244.

Paul Ylvisaker, "Foundations and Nonprofit Organizations," in *The Nonprofit Sector: A Research Handbook*, Yale University Press, 1987, pp. 363–364.

CHAPTER 9

Stanley N. Katz, "Problems in Private Foundation Support of Academic Research—the United States Experience," unpublished, p. 26.

Teresa Jean Odendahl, Elizabeth Trocolli Boris, Arlene Kaplan Daniels, *Working in Foundations*, The Foundation Center, 1985, p. 11.

CHAPTER 10

Donald R. Young, in *Trusteeship and the Management of Foundations*, by Donald R. Young and Wilbert E. Moore, Russell Sage Foundation, 1969, p. 41.

Waldemar A. Nielsen, *The Golden Donors*, E. P. Dutton, 1985, pp. 415–416.

CHAPTER 11

Foundations, Private Giving, and Public Policy, The Report of the Peterson Commission, University of Chicago Press, 1970, p. 124.

Richard Magat, "Hands On: Out of the Shadows," in *Foundation News*, July/August 1984, p. 24.

Frank Karel, "News Coverage: Refreshing and Candid," in *Increasing the Impact: 1980's*, W. K. Kellogg Foundation, 1985, p. 54.

CHAPTER 12

James A. Joseph, "1969–1983: From Abuse to Access—A Different Spotlight," in *Foundation News*, July/August 1983, p. 43.

Benjamin Cardozo, *Meinhard v. Salmon*, 249N.Y.458, 164N.E.545 (1928), 249N.Y. at 464, Cardozo, Chief Judge.

CHAPTER 13

Frederick T. Gates, in statement to the Rockefeller Foundation at his last board meeting, 1923.

Robert K. Greenleaf, "The Trustee: The Buck Starts Here," in *Foundation News*, July/August 1973, p. 30.

SELECT BIBLIOGRAPHY AND SUGGESTED READINGS

The following are books and special studies that were particularly helpful in the preparation of this manuscript. Also listed are several other resources of particular interest to foundation trustees.

Andrews, F. Emerson, *Philanthropic Foundations*, Russell Sage Foundation, 1956.

Andrews, F. Emerson (Ed.), *Foundations: 20 Viewpoints*, Russell Sage Foundation, 1965.

Bundy, McGeorge, *Foundation Trustees: Their Moral And Social Responsibility*, The Ford Foundation, 1975.

Commission on Foundations and Private Philanthropy (the Peterson Commission), *Foundations, Private Giving and Public Policy*, University of Chicago Press, 1970.

Commission on Private Philanthropy and Public Needs (the Filer Commission), *Giving in America*, 1975.

Congress and Private Foundations: An Historical Analysis (occasional paper), Council on Foundations, 1987.

Council on Foundations 1980 Trustee Report, Council on Foundations, 1980.

Cuninggim, Merrimon, *Private Money and Public Service: The Role of Foundations in American Society*, McGraw-Hill Book Company, 1972.

Directors and Officers Liability Insurance, Council on Foundations, 1984.

Donee Group, *Private Philanthropy: Vital & Innovative? or Passive & Irrelevant?*, 1975.

The Foundation Directory, Introduction to 11th Ed., The Foundation Center, 1987.

1988 Foundation Management Report, Council on Foundations, 1988.

Foundation News, magazine published bimonthly by the Council on Foundations.

Fremont-Smith, Marion R., *Foundations and Government: State and Federal Law and Supervision*, Russell Sage Foundation, 1965.

Giving USA, 1987, AAFRC Trust for Philanthropy, 1988.

Greenleaf, Robert K., *Trustees as Servants*, Center for Applied Studies, Cambridge, 1974.

Heimann, Fritz R. (Ed.), *The Future of Foundations*, Prentice-Hall, 1973.

Katz, Milton, *The Modern Foundation; Its Dual Character, Public and Private*, Foundation Library Center, 1968.

Merrill, Charles, *The Checkbook*, Oelgesch, Gunn, and Hain, 1986.

New Developments in Trustee Responsibilities: Legal Climate/Duty of Care, Council on Foundations, 1987 (audio tape).

New Developments in Trustee Responsibilities: Three Plenary Speeches, Council on Foundations, 1987 (audio tape).

Nielsen, Waldemar A., *The Golden Donors*, E. P. Dutton, 1985.

Nielsen, Waldemar A., *The Big Foundations*, Columbia University Press, 1972.

Odendahl, Teresa (Ed.), *America's Wealthy and the Future of Foundations*, The Foundation Center, 1987. Sponsored by the Council on Foundations and the Yale Program on Non-Profit Organizations.

Odendahl, Teresa, Elizabeth Boris, and Arlene Kaplan Daniels, *Working in Foundations*, The Foundation Center, 1985.

Pifer, Alan, *The Foundation in the Year 2000*, Foundation Library Center, 1968.

Pifer, Alan, *Philanthropy in an Age of Transition*, The Foundation Center, 1984.

Pifer, Alan, *Speaking Out: Reflections on 30 Years of Foundation Work*, Council on Foundations, 1984.

Powell, Walter (Ed.), *The Nonprofit Sector: A Research Handbook*, Yale University Press, 1987.

Self-Study Guide for Foundation Boards, Council on Foundations, 1986. A questionnaire and instructions on conducting a self-evaluation of a foundation and its board. Versions available for private family, private nonfamily, and community foundations.

Struckhoff, Eugene C., *The Handbook for Community Foundations: Their Formation, Development, and Operation*, Council on Foundations, Inc., 1977 (out of print).

Trustee Orientation Packet, Council on Foundations, 1987.

Young, Donald R., and Wilbert Moore, *Trusteeship and the Management of Foundations*, Russell Sage Foundation, 1969.

Zurcher, Arnold J., *Management of American Foundations: Administration, Policies and Social Rule*, New York University Press, 1972.

Zurcher, Arnold J., and Jane Dustan, *The Foundation Administrator: A Study of Those Who Manage America's Foundations*, Russell Sage Foundation, 1972.

The Filer Commission sponsored a considerable number of special studies in *Research Papers: The Commission on Private Philanthropy and Public Needs*, Volumes I–V. Department of the Treasury, 1977. Some of the most useful to foundation trustees are the following:

Asher, Tomas R., *Public Needs, Public Policy and Philanthropy*. Volume II, pp. 1069–1089.

Carey, Sarah C., *Philanthropy and the Powerless*. Volume II, pp. 1109–1157.

Council on Foundations, *Private Foundations and the 1969 Tax Reform Act*, Volume III, pp. 1557–1653.

Harris, James F., and Anne Klepper, *Corporate Philanthropic Public Service Activities*. Volume III, pp. 1741–1788.

Mavity, Jane H., and Paul Ylvisaker, *The Role of Private Philanthropy in Public Affairs*. Volume II, pp. 795–835.

Stone, Lawrence M., *The Charitable Foundation: Its Governance*. Volume III, pp. 1723–1734.

Index